New Headway

Beginner Student's Book

John and Liz Soars

OXFORD
UNIVERSITY PRESS

CONTENTS

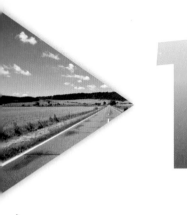

1

Hello!

am/are/is, my/your • This is . . . • How are you? • Good morning!
What's this in English? • Numbers 1–10 • Plurals

T 1.1 Listen. Say your name.

Hello. I'm Paula.

Hello. I'm Josef.

WHAT'S YOUR NAME?
am/are/is, my/your

1 **T 1.2** Read and listen.

> **Pablo** Hello. I'm Pablo. What's your name?
> **Mika** My name's Mika.
> **Pablo** Hello, Mika.

T 1.2 Listen and repeat.

GRAMMAR SPOT

I'**m** = I am
name'**s** = name is
What'**s** = What is

2 Stand up and practise.

Hello. I'm _____ .
What's your name?

My name's _____ .

INTRODUCTIONS
This is . . .

1 [T 1.3] Read and listen.

Pablo	Ben, this is Mika. Mika, this is Ben.
Mika	Hello, Ben.
Ben	Hello, Mika.

[T 1.3] Listen and repeat.

2 Practise in groups of three.

_____ , this is _____ .
_____ , this is _____ .
Hello, _____ .
Hello, _____ .

Nice to meet you

3 [T 1.4] Read and listen.

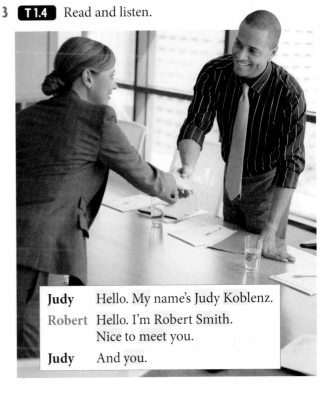

Judy	Hello. My name's Judy Koblenz.
Robert	Hello. I'm Robert Smith. Nice to meet you.
Judy	And you.

[T 1.4] Listen and repeat.

4 Practise in pairs. Say your first name and surname.

A Hello. My name's _____ _____ .

B Hello. I'm _____ _____ . Nice to meet you.

A And you.

5 [T 1.5] Listen to the English names.

♂	James Bond	Robert Taylor	Henry Baker
♀	Susie Walsh	Anita Johnson	Katherine Smith

Choose a name. Stand up and say hello.

HOW ARE YOU?

1 **T 1.6** Read and listen.

1 Pablo Hi, Ben. How are you? **Ben** Fine, thanks, Pablo. And you? **Pablo** I'm OK, thanks.	**2 Ben** Hello, Mika. How are you? **Mika** Very well, thank you. How are you? **Ben** Fine.

T 1.6 Listen and repeat.

2 Answer your teacher.

Hi, _____ . How are you?

Fine, thanks.

Fine, thanks. And you?

3 Stand up and practise.

Very well, thank you.

OK, thanks.

GRAMMAR SPOT

Write *'m*, *is*, or *are*.

I ____ Sandra.   How ____ you?   This ____ John.

▶▶ **Grammar Reference 1.1–1.3 p123**

---

4 Complete the conversations.

1

A Hello. __My____ name's Ana.
_____ your name?
B _____ _____ Mario.

2

A Max, _____ is Carla.
B Hi, Carla.
C Hello, Max. _____ to meet you.

3

A Hi, Eda. _____ are you?
B Fine, thanks, David.
And _____ ?
A _____ well, thanks.

T 1.7 Listen and check. Practise the conversations.

EVERYDAY ENGLISH
Good morning!

1 Complete the conversations.

| Goodbye! | Good night! | ~~Good morning!~~ | Good afternoon! |

1 A _Good morning!_
  B Good morning!
    What a lovely day!

2 A _____
  B Hello. A cup of tea, please.

3 A _____
  B Bye! See you later!

4 A _____
  B Good night! Sleep well!

T1.8 Listen and check. Practise the conversations.

2 Put the words in the correct order.

1 A Good morning!
  | are | you | How | today |
    How are you today ?
  B Fine, thanks.

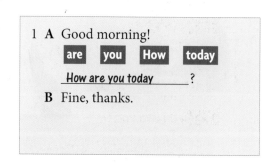

2 A Good afternoon!
  B Good afternoon!
    | coffee | cup | please | of | A |
    _____ , _____ .

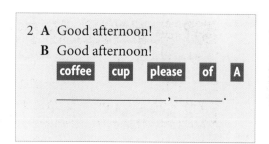

3 A Goodbye!
  | nice | Have | day | a |
    _____ .
  B Thank you. And you.
    | you | later | See |
    _____ .

4 A Good night!
  | well | Sleep |
    _____ !
  B Thank you.
    | you | And |
    _____ .

T1.9 Listen and check. Practise the conversations.

VOCABULARY AND SPEAKING
What's this in English?

1 Write the words.

1 a book

2

3

4

5

a book
a camera
a car
a photograph
a computer
a bag
a hamburger
a television
a phone
a sandwich
a bus
a house

6

7

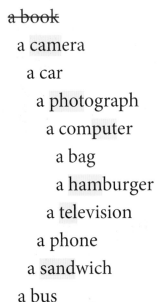

8

9

10

11

12

2 [T 1.10] Listen and repeat the words.

3 [T 1.11] Listen and repeat.

What's this in English?

It's a photograph.

Work with a partner. Point to a picture. Ask and answer questions.

4 Go to things in the room. Ask your teacher.

What's this in English?

It's a ...

Numbers 1–10 and plurals

1 **T 1.12** Read and listen. Practise the numbers.

1 one

2 two

3 three

4 four

5 five

6 six

7 seven

8 eight

9 nine

10 ten

2 Say the numbers round the class.

3 Write the numbers.

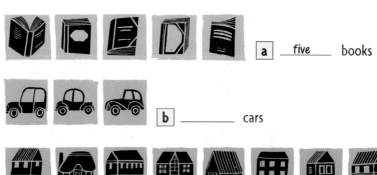

a ___five___ books

b _____ cars

c _____ houses

d _____ cameras

e _____ photographs

f _____ sandwiches

g _____ computers

h _____ buses

i _____ students

T 1.13 Listen and check.

4 Ask and answer questions.

> What's in this picture?

> Nine photographs.

5 **T 1.14** Listen and repeat.

/s/	/z/	/ɪz/
books	cars	sandwiches
photographs	computers	houses
students	hamburgers	buses
	cameras	
	televisions	
	bags	
	phones	

GRAMMAR SPOT

Singular	Plural
one book	two books
one bus	two buses

▶▶ **Grammar reference 1.4 p123**

2 Your world

Countries • *he/she/they, his/her* • Where's he from?
fantastic/awful/beautiful • Numbers 11–30

STARTER

Find your country on the map on page 13. Find these countries on the map.

| Australia | Brazil | Egypt | China | England | France | Italy | Hungary | Japan | Russia | Spain | the United States |

T 2.1 Listen and repeat.

SHE'S FROM JAPAN
he/she, his/her

1 **T 2.2** Read and listen.

Pablo Where are you from, Mika?
Mika I'm from Japan. Where are you from?
Pablo I'm from Spain. From Barcelona.

T 2.2 Listen and repeat.

2 Where are you from? Stand up and practise.

> Where are you from?

> I'm from Italy/Brazil ... Where ... ?

3 **T 2.3** Read, listen, and repeat.

His name's Pablo. He's from Spain.

Her name's Mika. She's from Japan.

GRAMMAR SPOT

he's = he is   she's = she is

▶▶ Grammar Reference 2.1–2.2 p123

QUESTIONS
Where's he from?

1 Complete the sentences about the people.

1 _His_ name's Kevin. He's _from the United States_.

2 _____ name's László. He's _____.

3 _____ name's Karima. She's _____.

4 _____ name's Tatiana. She's _____.

5 _____ name's Rosely. She's _____.

6 _____ name's Simon. He's _____.

7 _____ name's Yong. He's _____.

8 _____ name's Hayley. She's _____.

T 2.4 Listen and check. Repeat the sentences.

2 **T 2.5** Listen and repeat the questions.

What's his name?	Where's he from?
What's her name?	Where's she from?

?

3 Ask and answer questions about the people in the photographs.

What's his name?

His name's Kevin.

Where's he from?

He's from the United States.

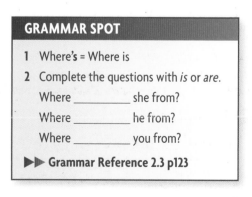

GRAMMAR SPOT

1 Where's = Where is

2 Complete the questions with *is* or *are*.
Where _____ she from?
Where _____ he from?
Where _____ you from?

▶▶ **Grammar Reference 2.3 p123**

PRACTICE

Cities and countries

1 Where are the cities? Ask and answer.

> Where's Barcelona?

> It's in Spain.

Barcelona	**São Paulo**
Beijing	**Sydney**
Moscow	**Tokyo**
Cairo	**Budapest**
Los Angeles	**London**

 Listen and check.

2 Work with a partner.

Student A Look at the photos on this page.
Student B Look at the photos on p140.

Ask questions and write the answers.

> What's his/her name?

> Where's he/she from?

Talking about you

3 Ask about the students in the class.

> What's his name?

> His name's Marco.

> Where's he from?

> He's from Italy. From Rome.

> What's her name?

> Her name's Donatella.

> Where's she from?

> She's from Rome, too.

Her name's Shu-fei.
She's from Beijing.

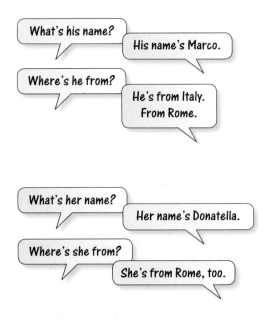

His name's Adam.
He's from Sydney.

His name's Andrei.
He's from Moscow.

Her name's Ashlee.
She's from Los Angeles.

_____
_____

Questions and answers

4 **T 2.7** Listen and complete the conversation. Practise it.

> **Rosely** Hello, I'm Rosely. What's _your_____ name?
>
> **Bruno** _____ name's Bruno.
>
> **R** Hello, Bruno. Where are you _____?
>
> **B** _____ from Brazil. Where are you from?
>
> **R** Oh, I'm from Brazil, too. _____ from São Paulo.
>
> **B** Really? I'm from São Paulo, too!
>
> **R** Oh, nice to meet you, Bruno.

5 **T 2.8** Listen and write the countries.

1 Claudio: ___Italy___ Akemi: _____

2 Charles: _____ Bud: _____

3 Loretta and Jason: _____

6 Match the questions and answers.

1	d	Where are you from?	a His name's Bruno.
2	☐	What's her name?	b He's from São Paulo.
3	☐	What's his name?	c It's in Canada.
4	☐	Where's he from?	d I'm from Brazil.
5	☐	What's this in English?	e Fine, thanks.
6	☐	How are you?	f Her name's Tatiana.
7	☐	Where's Montreal?	g It's a computer.

T 2.9 Listen and check.

Work with a partner. Take turns to cover the questions or the answers. Practise them.

Check it

7 Tick (✓) the correct sentence.

1 ☐ My name Mika.
  ✓ My name's Mika.

2 ☐ What's he's name?
  ☐ What's his name?

3 ☐ 'What's his name?' 'Kevin.'
  ☐ 'What's her name?' 'Kevin.'

4 ☐ He's from Spain.
  ☐ His from Spain.

5 ☐ Where she from?
  ☐ Where's she from?

6 ☐ What's her name?
  ☐ What's she name?

READING AND SPEAKING
Where are they from?

1 **T 2.10** Read and listen.

This is a photograph of **Claude** and **Holly Duval** from Montreal in Canada. They are on holiday in New York City. Holly is from Canada and Claude is from France. They are married. Holly is a teacher. Her school is in the centre of Montreal. Claude is a doctor. His hospital is in the centre of Montreal, too.

2 Complete the sentences.

1 Holly is from _____ in Canada.
2 She's a _____ .
3 Her _____ is in the centre of Montreal.
4 Claude is from _____ .
5 He's a _____ .
6 His hospital is in the _____ of Montreal.
7 They _____ in New York.
8 They are _____ .

3 Write questions with *What ... ?* and *Where ... ?* about Claude and Holly. Ask a partner.

What ... name? *Where ... from?*
Where ... school? *Where ... hospital?*

GRAMMAR SPOT

Write *is* or *are*.
She _____ a teacher.
He _____ a doctor.
They _____ from Canada.

▶▶ **Grammar reference 2.4 p123**

---

4 **T 2.11** Listen to Claude and Holly. Complete the conversations.

1 `awful` ☹ `weather`
   C Oh, no! Look at the __weather__ !
   H Ugh! It's _____ !

2 `really good` ☺ `hamburger`
   H Wow! Look at my _____ !
      It's fantastic!
   C My hamburger is _____ , too!

3 `fantastic` ☺ `building`
   C What's this __building__ ?
   H It's the Empire State Building!
      It's _____ !

4 `beautiful` ☺ `Look`
   C Wow! _____ at Central Park!
   H It's _____ !

T 2.11 Listen and check. Practise the conversations.

EVERYDAY ENGLISH
Numbers 11–30

1 Say the numbers 1–10 round the class.

2 **T 2.12** Listen, read, and repeat.

11	**12**	**13**	**14**	**15**
eleven	twelve	thirteen	fourteen	fifteen

16	**17**	**18**	**19**	**20**
sixteen	seventeen	eighteen	nineteen	twenty

Say the numbers 1–20 round the class.

3 Write the numbers your teacher says. Say the numbers your teacher writes.

4 Match the numbers.

21	twenty-five
22	twenty-seven
23	twenty-one
24	twenty-eight
25	twenty-two
26	twenty-four
27	twenty-nine
28	twenty-three
29	thirty
30	twenty-six

T 2.13 Listen and repeat. Say the numbers 1–30 round the class.

5 **T 2.14** Listen and tick (✓) the numbers you hear.

1 22   12✓   10   20
2 17   15   16   14
3 21   29   19   9
4 11   7   17   27
5 23   3   13   30

6 Work with a partner.
Student A Write five numbers. Say them to your partner.
Student B Write the numbers you hear. *14 24 …*

7 Look at the pictures. How old is he/she?

> I think she's 18 months.

> No, I think she's about 2.

T 2.15 Listen and find out.

3 All about you

Jobs • *am/are/is* • Negatives and questions • Personal information • Social expressions (1)

1 Match the jobs and the pictures.

| a doctor   a nurse   a student   ~~a teacher~~   a shop assistant |
| a bus driver   a businessman   a police officer   a builder |

1 a teacher

2

3

4

5

6

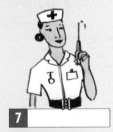

7

8

9

T 3.1 Listen and repeat.

2 **T 3.2** Read the questions and answers. Listen and repeat.

What's his job?　　He's a teacher.

What's her job?　　She's a doctor.

Look at the pictures. Ask and answer questions with a partner.

3 What's your job? Ask and answer.

What's your job?

I'm a student.

I'm a businessman.

HE ISN'T A STUDENT
Negatives – *he isn't*

1 Look and read.

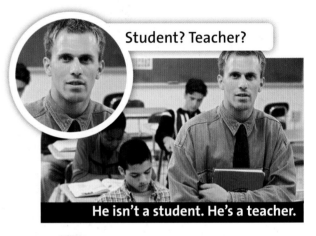

Student? Teacher?

He isn't a student. He's a teacher.

Nurse? Doctor?

She isn't a nurse. She's a doctor.

T 3.3 Listen and repeat.

2 Look at pictures 1–9 again.
Make more negative and positive sentences.

He/She isn't a . . .　　He/She's a . . .

GRAMMAR SPOT	
He's a teacher.	's = is
She isn't a nurse.	isn't = is not

PERSONAL INFORMATION
Questions and answers

1 Look at the photos and read Ellie's profile.

friendspace   **PROFILE**

Ellie Green

Surname:	Green
First name:	Ellie
Country:	England
Address:	29, Victoria Road, Birmingham
Phone number:	07700 955031
Age:	20
Job:	Student
Married:	No

Ellie's Photos ◀ • • • ● • ▶

2 Complete the questions and answers.

1 What's her **surname** ?   Green

2 What's her _____ ?   Ellie

3 Where's she _____ ?   England

4 What's her _____ ?   29, Victoria Road, Birmingham

5 What's her _____ ?   07700 955031

6 How old is she?   She's _____ .

7 What's _____ ?   She's _____ .

8 Is she _____ ?   No, she isn't.

T 3.4 Listen and check. Practise the questions and answers.

3 **T 3.5** Read and listen. Then listen and repeat.

Is Ellie from America?	✗ No, she isn't.
Is she from Spain?	✗ No, she isn't.
Is she from England?	✓ Yes, she is.

4 Ask and answer questions about Ellie.

1 Is she from London? Liverpool? Birmingham?
2 Is she 16? 18? 20?
3 Is she a teacher? a nurse? a student?
4 Is she married?

5 Complete the sentences.

1 Ellie **isn't** from the United States.
   She **'s** from England.

2 Her phone number _____ 07700 995031.
   It _____ 07700 955031.

3 She _____ 18. She _____ 20.

4 She _____ married.

METRO 5 – THE AUDITION

Negatives – *I'm not, they aren't*

1 Look at the picture. Who are the people?

2 **T 3.6** Listen to and read **The Audition Interview**. Listen again and complete the questions.

3 Answer the questions about the band.

1 What's the band's name?
2 Are Paul and Donny brothers?
3 Are they from Scotland?
4 Are the other boys from Ireland?
5 Are they all builders?
6 Are they all singers?

T 3.7 Listen and check. Practise the questions and answers.

GRAMMAR SPOT

1 Negative
I'm not from Scotland. **I'm not** = I am not
They aren't from Ireland. **They aren't** = They are not.

2 Short answers
Are you from Scotland? **Yes, I am./No, I'm not.**
Is this your band? **Yes, it is./No, it isn't.**
Are they from Ireland? **Yes, they are./No, they aren't.**

▶▶ **Grammar reference 3.1 p124**

---

4 Practise **The Audition Interview** in groups of three.

Talking about you

5 Ask and answer the questions about you.

Are you from Ireland?

Are you a student?

Yes, . . .

Are you a nurse?

No, . . .

Are you married?

Are the other students from Ireland?

Are they married?

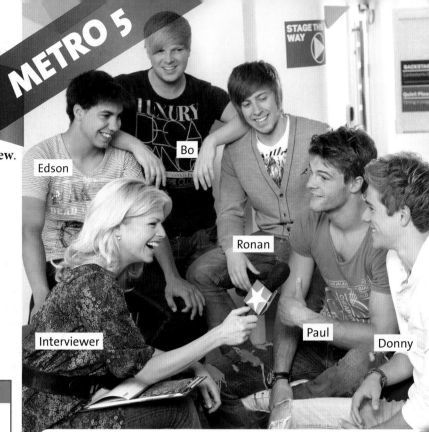

Edson
Bo
Ronan
Interviewer
Paul
Donny

THE AUDITION
INTERVIEW

I	Hi! <u>Is</u> <u>this</u> your band, *Metro 5*?
P	Yes, it is.
I	Great! And _____ _____ Donny McNab?
P	No, I'm not. I'm Paul McNab. This is Donny. He's my brother.
I	Ah, yes, sorry. Hi, Donny. You're a builder from Scotland, right?
D	Well, yes, I am a builder, but I'm not from Scotland.
I	Oh, where _____ _____ from?
P&D	We're from Ireland.
I	Aah! _____ the other boys from Ireland too?
D	No, they aren't. They're all from different countries.
I	Oh! Interesting! And _____ _____ all builders?
D	No, they aren't. Paul's a bus driver and . . .
P	Yeah, I'm a bus driver and Ronan's a nurse and Bo and Edson are students.
I	Interesting! And Donny, _____ _____ the singer in the band?
D	Yes, I am. Well, we're all singers.
I	Oh, right! Nice to meet you. Good luck to you all!
All	Thank you very much.

PRACTICE

Is he a businessman?

1 Look at the pictures of Diego and Grace. Where are they?

2 **T 3.8** Listen to the conversations. Complete the chart.

First name	Diego	Grace
Surname	Hernandez	Chou
Country	Mexico	
City/Town		
Phone number		212 638-9475
Age	42	
Job		Shop assistant
Married?		

T 3.8 Listen again and check.

3 Ask and answer the questions with a partner.

- Is **Diego** from Mexico City? Yes, he is.
- Is he a businessman?
- Is he 42?
- Is he married?

- Is **Grace** from the United States?
- Is she a nurse?
- Is she 33?
- Is she married?

4 Talk about Diego and Grace.

> Diego is from Mexico City. His surname is ...

> Grace is from ...

Talking about you

5 Complete the questions.

1 <u>What's</u> <u>your</u> first name?
2 _____ _____ surname?
3 _____ _____ you from?
4 _____ _____ phone number?
5 How old _____ _____ ?
6 _____ _____ job?
7 _____ _____ married?

In groups, ask and answer the questions.

Writing

6 Write about another student. Read it aloud.

Her name's ...   She's from Italy...   Her phone number is ...

Check it

7 Tick (✓) the correct sentence.

1 ☐ She's name's Anna.
   ✓ Her name's Anna.
2 ☐ Her job is teacher.
   ☐ She's a teacher.
3 ☐ He's phone number is 796542.
   ☐ His phone number is 796542.
4 ☐ I'm not a doctor.
   ☐ I amn't a doctor.
5 ☐ They aren't from Italy.
   ☐ They're no from Italy.
6 ☐ She is no married.
   ☐ She isn't married.

READING AND LISTENING
We're in Las Vegas!

1 Read the magazine article about the band, *Metro 5*.

METRO 5
ON TOUR IN LAS VEGAS

This is the boy band *Metro 5* – The Audition winners. They are from different countries. Paul and Donny McNab are from Ireland, they are brothers. Bo Olsson is from Sweden. Ronan Wilson is from Australia, and Edson Melo is from Brazil.
Now they are on tour in the United States.

Metro 5	Hi! We're in Las Vegas.
Interviewer	Hi, guys, how are you?
Metro 5	We're all fine. It's fantastic here!
Interviewer	Are you tired?
Metro 5	No, we aren't. We're very happy and excited.
Interviewer	Great! Good luck with the tour!

GRAMMAR SPOT

We're in Las Vegas.   **we're** = we are
We aren't tired.   **we aren't** = we are not

▶▶ **Grammar Reference 3.2 p124**

2 Answer the questions.
1 Are all the boys from Ireland?
2 Are they all brothers?
3 Where are they?
4 Are they happy?

3 Read about the band again. Correct the information.

1 The band, *Metro 5*, are in Brazil.
   They aren't in Brazil! They're in the United States!

2 They're in New York.
   _____ .

3 Bo's from Australia.
   _____ .

4 Edson's from Sweden.
   _____ .

5 They're very tired.
   _____ .

T 3.9 Listen and check. Practise the lines.

Interview with the band

4 **T 3.10** Listen. Answer the questions.
1 How old is Ronan?
2 Who is 21?
3 How old are Paul and Donny?
4 Who is married? Who isn't married?

Roleplay

5 Work in groups of four. You are a band.
- What's the name of the band?
- What are your names?
- Where are you from?
- How old are you?
- Where are you now?

Ask and answer the questions with another group.

EVERYDAY ENGLISH
Social expressions (1)

1 [T 3.11] Listen and look at the pictures.

OK   sorry
1 **A** I'm **sorry** .
B That's _____.

Thanks   please
2 **C** A coffee, _____ .
D That's £1.20.
C _____ very much.

Excuse   a lot   over there
3 **E** _____ me!
Where's the station?
F It's _____.
E Thanks _____ .

kind   very much   OK
4 **G** Thank you _____ .
That's very _____ .
H That's _____ .

don't understand   sorry
5 **I** *¿Qué hora es?*
J I'm _____ . I _____ .

don't know   Excuse
6 **K** _____ me!
Where's the town centre?
L I'm sorry. I _____ .

2 Complete the conversations with the words in the boxes.
[T 3.11] Listen again and check.

3 Work with a partner. Learn the conversations.
Stand up! Act the conversations.

4 Family and friends

our/their • Possessive *'s* • The family • *has/have* • The alphabet

1 Complete the chart.

I	you	he	she	we	they
my				our	their

2 Talk about things in the classroom.

> This is my book.

> This is our class.

> This is her bag.

MY FAMILY
Possessive *'s*

1 **T 4.1** Read and listen.

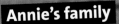

Annie's family

ANNIE TAYLOR

This is Annie Taylor. She's married, and this is her family. Their house is in London. She's a doctor. Annie's hospital is in the centre of town.

Jim is Annie's husband. He's a bank manager. Jim's office is in the centre of town, too.

'Our children are Emma and Vince. Emma is 15, she's at Camden High School. Vince is 19, he's at the University of Westminster. We're all happy in London.'

Annie

Jim

Emma

Vince

GRAMMAR SPOT

1   She's married.   She's a doctor.   's = is
2   This is her family.
    This is **Annie's** family   's = the family of Annie
3   his | office
    Jim's |
    her | school
    Emma's |
▶▶ **Grammar Reference 4.1–4.3 p124**

2 Answer the questions.

1 Is Annie married?   <u>Yes, she is</u> .
2 Where's their house?   _____ .
3 What's Annie's job?   _____ .
4 Where's her hospital?   _____ .
5 What's Jim's job?   _____ .
6 Are their children both at school?   _____ .

T 4.2   Listen, check, and practise.

Annie's hospital

Who are they?

3 **T 4.3**   Listen and repeat.

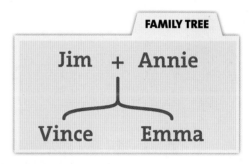

♀	mother	daughter	sister	wife
♂	father	son	brother	husband
👥	parents	children

4 Look at the family tree.

FAMILY TREE

Jim + Annie

Vince   Emma

T 4.4   Listen and complete the sentences.

1 Annie is Jim's _wife_ .
2 Jim is Annie's _____ .
3 Emma is Annie and Jim's _____ .
4 Vince is their _____ .
5 Annie is Vince's _____ .
6 Jim is Emma's _____ .
7 Emma is Vince's _____ .
8 Vince is Emma's _____ .
9 Annie and Jim are Emma and Vince's _____ .
10 Emma and Vince are Jim and Annie's _____ .

T 4.4   Listen again and check.

5 Ask and answer questions with a partner.

> Who's Vince?
>
> He's Emma's brother.
>
> He's Jim's son.

6 **T 4.5**   Listen to the five people. Who are they?

1 <u>Annie</u>   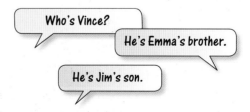 Come on, Emma! Time for school!
2 _____
3 _____
4 _____
5 _____

PRACTICE

An American family

1 **T 4.6** Listen to Elena Díaz from Chicago.
Complete the information about her family.

	Name	Age	Job
Elena's brother	Oscar		
Elena's mother			
Elena's father			

2 Complete the sentences.

1 Oscar is __Elena's__ brother.
2 Her _____ name is Maria.
3 'What's _____ job?' 'He's a businessman.'
4 'Where's _____ house?' 'It's in Chicago.'

3 Write the names of people in your family.

__Stefan__   __Danuta__

Ask and answer questions with a partner.

> Who's Stefan/Danuta?

> He's/She's my brother/mother ...

> How old is he/she?

> He's/She's ...

> What's his/her job?

> He's/She's a ...

my / our / your . . .

4 Complete the sentences with *my, our, your, …*

1 'What's your name?'
  '__My__ name's Annie.'
2 'What are _____ names?'
  'Our names are Emma and Vince.'
3 Jean-Paul and André are students.
  _____ school is in Paris.
4 'My sister's married.'
  'What's _____ husband's name?'
5 'My brother's office is in New York.'
  'What's _____ job?'
6 We're in _____ English class.
7 'Mum and Dad are in Rome.'
  'What's the name of _____ hotel?'

T 4.7 Listen and check.

ANNIE'S BROTHER
has/have

1 Look at the picture. Who are the people?
T 4.8 Read and listen to Paddy.

2 Are the sentences true (✓) or false (✗)?

1 ✗ Paddy's hotel is in England.
   It isn't in England. It's in Ireland.

2 ✓ His wife has a job in a hospital.

3 ☐ Annie is Paddy's wife.

4 ☐ Their hotel is very big.

5 ☐ Paddy and Shona have three children.

6 ☐ All their sons are in Las Vegas.

7 ☐ Jim and Annie have a son and a daughter.

Donny
Conor
Paul
Paddy
Shona

**Paddy McNab
and his family**

'We're from Ireland. I have a small hotel in the city of Galway. My wife's name is Shona, and she has a job as a nurse in a hospital near the town centre.
We have three sons, Paul, Donny, and Conor. We have an apartment in the hotel. Our sons Paul and Donny have a band, *Metro 5*. They're in Las Vegas now. Conor is here with us. My sister, Annie, and her husband, Jim, have a big house in London. They have two children, a son and a daughter. Annie has a very good job. Jim has a good job, too.'

GRAMMAR SPOT

Complete the forms of the verb *have*.

I	_have_	We	_____
You	_____	They	_____
He	_has_		
She	_____		

▶▶ **Grammar Reference 4.4 p124**

---

3 **T 4.9** Listen and complete the sentences. Practise them.

1 _I have a small hotel_____ in the city of Galway.

2 _____ in town.

3 _____ three sons.

4 _____ called *Metro 5*.

5 _____ house in London.

4 Write sentences about your family. Tell the class.

> **We have a house in the centre of town.**

> **I have two sisters.**

PRACTICE

has/have

1 Complete the sentences. Use *has* or *have*.

1 I _have_ two brothers and a sister.
2 My parents _____ a house in the country.
3 My wife _____ a Japanese car.
4 My sister and I _____ a dog.
5 You _____ a very nice family.
6 Our school _____ fifteen classrooms.
7 We _____ English classes in the evening.

2 Talk about your school.

> Our school is fantastic!

> It has six classrooms.

> We have ten students in our class.

Questions and answers

3 Match the questions and answers.

1	[d] How is your mother?	a	Smith.
2	[ ] What's your sister's job?	b	He's a student from Madrid.
3	[ ] How old are your daughters?	c	It's in the centre of town.
4	[ ] Who is Pedro?	d	She's very well, thank you.
5	[ ] Where's your office?	e	They're ten and thirteen.
6	[ ] What's your surname?	f	She's a nurse.

T 4.10 Listen, check, and practise.

Check it

4 Tick (✓) the correct sentence.

1 ✓ Mary's children are married.
   [ ] Mary is children are married.
2 [ ] What's your daughter name?
   [ ] What's your daughter's name?
3 [ ] What's he's job?
   [ ] What's his job?
4 [ ] They're from Germany.
   [ ] Their from Germany.
5 [ ] They're parents have a house in Bonn.
   [ ] Their parents have a house in Bonn.
6 [ ] My brother have a good job.
   [ ] My brother has a good job.
7 [ ] We have a lovely teacher.
   [ ] We has a lovely teacher.

READING AND WRITING
My best friend

1 Read about Antonia. Check the new words in your dictionary.

2 Match the photos with a part of the text. Who are the people in the photos?

My friend Antonia

a My best friend's name is Antonia – Toni for short. She's very beautiful, and she's really funny. She's 18, and she's a student at university in London. She has a lot of friends and a great boyfriend. His name is Vince, he's 19 and he's also at university.

b Toni is from the north of England. Her parents have a house in a village near Manchester. Her father is an accountant, and her mother has a part-time job in a bank.

c She has a brother and a sister. Their names are Mark and Alison. Mark is 16 and Alison is 14. They're both at school.

d Toni has a lot of music. Her favourite music is rock 'n' roll, and her favourite band is *Metro 5*. She likes dancing. She and Alison like dancing a lot. She also likes football. She and her brother, Mark, are big Manchester United fans.

When we're together, we have a really good time.

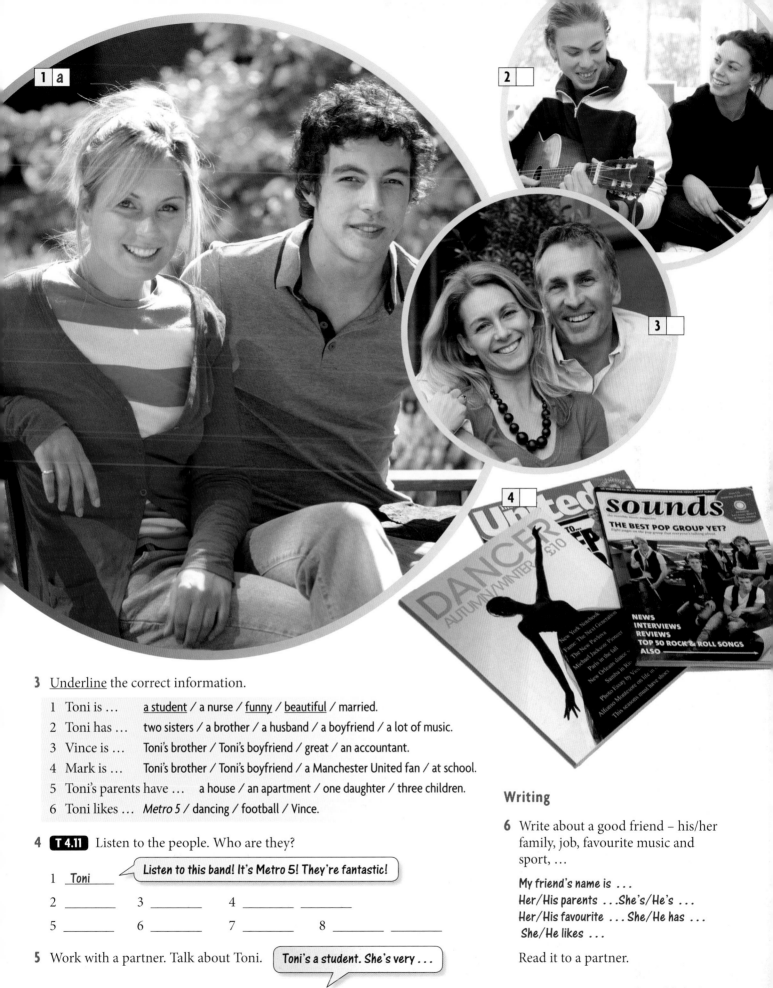

3 <u>Underline</u> the correct information.

1 Toni is … <u>a student</u> / a nurse / <u>funny</u> / <u>beautiful</u> / married.

2 Toni has … two sisters / a brother / a husband / a boyfriend / a lot of music.

3 Vince is … Toni's brother / Toni's boyfriend / great / an accountant.

4 Mark is … Toni's brother / Toni's boyfriend / a Manchester United fan / at school.

5 Toni's parents have … a house / an apartment / one daughter / three children.

6 Toni likes … *Metro 5* / dancing / football / Vince.

4 **T 4.11** Listen to the people. Who are they?

1 <u>Toni</u> ┌─────────────────────────────────────┐
            │ Listen to this band! It's Metro 5! They're fantastic! │
            └─────────────────────────────────────┘

2 _____ 3 _____ 4 _____ _____

5 _____ 6 _____ 7 _____ 8 _____ _____

5 Work with a partner. Talk about Toni. ┌────────────────────────────┐
                                            │ Toni's a student. She's very … │
                                            └────────────────────────────┘

Writing

6 Write about a good friend – his/her family, job, favourite music and sport, …

My friend's name is …
Her/His parents …She's/He's …
Her/His favourite …She/He has …
She/He likes …

Read it to a partner.

EVERYDAY ENGLISH
The alphabet

Aa Bb Cc Dd Ee Ff
Gg Hh Ii Jj Kk Ll Mm
Nn Oo Pp Qq Rr Ss
Tt Uu Vv Ww Xx Yy Zz

1 Look at the letters of the alphabet.
T 4.12 Listen. Practise them.

2 **T 4.13** Listen and practise the groups of letters.

/eɪ/	a h j k	/əʊ/	o
/iː/	b c d e g p t v	/uː/	q u w
/e/	f l m n s x z	/ɑː/	r
/aɪ/	i y		

How do you spell . . . ?

3 **T 4.14** Listen to people spell their first name (*Annie*) and their surname (*Taylor*). Write the names.

1 _ANNIE_ _TAYLOR_
2 _____ _____
3 _____ _____
4 _____ _____
5 _____ _____ _____

4 Practise spelling your name with a partner.

How do you spell your first name? A-N-T-O-N-I-A

How do you spell your surname? D-O-W-N-I-N-G

5 Work with a partner. Ask and answer *How do you spell . . . ?* with words from the text about Antonia on p28.

How do you spell 'friend'? F-R-I-E-N-D

6 Put the letters in the correct order. What's the country?

N E F A C R _FRANCE_
N A P I S _____
L A R Z I B _____
N A P A J _____
L A S A R U T A I _____
Y L I A T _____
G A N E L D N _____

7 Read the letters aloud. What are they?

VW UK NYPD
BBC US PC
WWW UAE TV

T 4.15 Listen and check.

On the phone

1 **T 4.16** Listen to two phone conversations and look at the business cards.

Conversation 1

A Good morning. Laxcon International.

J Hello. The Manager, please.

A Certainly. And your name is?

J José Gonzalez.

A How do you spell your surname?

J G – O – N – Z – A – L – E – Z.

A Thank you. I'm connecting you.

…

S Hello. Sam Benting speaking.

J Good morning, Mr Benting. My name's …

Conversation 2

B Good afternoon. The King School of English.

M Hello. Can you give me some information about your school, please?

B Of course. Your name is?

M Mayumi Morioka.

B Mayumi … Sorry, how do you spell your surname?

M M – O – R – I – O – K – A.

B Thank you. What's your email address?

M It's morioka@mmdesign.co.jp.

B I'll email you some information today.

M Thank you very much. Goodbye.

2 **T 4.16** Listen again and answer the questions.

1 What company is he/she phoning?
2 What does he/she want?
3 How do you spell his/her surname?
4 What's his/her email address?

Practise the conversations.

Email addresses

3 Notice how we say email addresses.

@ at	. dot	**com** /kɒm/	**co** /kəʊ/

uk /juː ˈkeɪ/ (United Kingdom)	**ca** /siː eɪ/ (Canada)

.it
.au
.es
.fr
wannado

hotmail
btinternet
compuserve
yahoo
.cz

4 **T 4.17** Listen and complete the email addresses.

1 pam_____@btinternet_____
2 harrylime_____
3 paul_____wannado_____
4 glennamiles_____

What's your email address? Tell a partner.

Roleplay

5 Write your business card.
Have conversations with a partner.
Phone the bank / a hotel / a sports centre …

	company name
name:	
address:	
tel:	fax:
email:	

5

The way I live

Sports/Food/Drinks • Present Simple – *I/you/we/they* • *a/an*
Languages and nationalities • Numbers and prices

1 Match the words and pictures.

| football | hamburger | skiing | wine | Chinese food | ~~tennis~~ | pizza |
| oranges | Coke | tea | swimming | ice-cream | coffee | Italian food | beer |

SPORTS

| 1 | tennis | 2 | | 3 | | 4 | |

FOOD

| 5 | | 6 | | 7 | |

| 8 | | 9 | | 10 | |

DRINKS

| 11 | | 12 | | 13 | | 14 | | 15 | |

T 5.1 Listen and repeat.

2 Tick (✓) the things you like. ☺   Cross (✗) the things you don't like. ☹

THINGS I LIKE
Present Simple

1 **T 5.2** Listen and repeat.

☺ I like ice-cream.

☺ I like football.

2 Say three things *you* like from pictures 1–15.

I like swimming, pizza, and beer.

Negatives

3 **T 5.3** Listen and repeat.

☹ I don't like tennis.

☹ I don't like coffee.

4 Say three things *you* don't like from pictures 1–15 on p32.

I don't like oranges, coffee, or tea.

GRAMMAR SPOT

Positive	I **like** ice-cream.	
Negative	I **don't like** tennis.	**don't** = do not

---

5 **T 5.4** Listen to Harvey. Complete his sentences.

HARVEY

SPORTS

'I like __sports__ a lot. I like _____ and _____ but I don't like _____ and I don't like _____ very much.'

FOOD AND DRINK

'I like __hamburgers__ and _____. And I like _____ food a lot. But I don't like _____ food and I don't like _____. I like _____ and I love _____.'

Questions *I, you, we, they*

6 **T 5.5** Listen and repeat.

Do you **like** football? **Yes, I do.**
Do you **like** tennis? **No, I don't.**

7 Work with a partner. Ask and answer about sports, food, and drinks.

Do you like football?

Yes, I do.

Do you like tennis?

No, I don't, but I like swimming.

8 **T 5.6** Harvey has a twin sister, Eva. Listen to them. What do they like? (✓) What don't they like? (✗) What do they say? Write the adjectives.

exciting
~~delicious~~
great
fantastic
awful

		HARVEY	EVA	
1	pizza	✓	✓	_delicious_
2	ice-cream	___	___	_____
3	tea	___	___	_____
4	skiing	___	___	_____
5	football	___	___	_____ _____

9 Talk about Harvey and Eva with a partner. What do they like?

They like pizza and . . .

GRAMMAR SPOT

Positive	I/You/We/They **like** football.
Question	What **do** you/they **like**? **Do** you/they **like** . . .?
Short answers	Yes, I/we/they **do**. No, I/we/they **don't**.
▶▶ Grammar Reference 5.1 p125	

PRACTICE

Reading and speaking

1 Look at the pictures. What's Colin's job?

T 5.7 Read and listen to the text.

COLIN BRODIE FROM DUNDEE

'Hello! My name's Colin Brodie. I come from Dundee in Scotland, but now I live and work in London. I have a very small flat near the centre. I live there with two friends. I'm a waiter and I'm also a drama student. I work part-time in an Italian restaurant. I eat Italian food and I drink Italian and French wine. I don't drink beer. I don't like it. I speak two languages – Spanish and French, but I don't speak Italian. And I don't play sports. I want to be an actor.'

2 **T 5.8** Listen to the conversation with Colin. Complete his answers.

	Questions	Colin's answers
1	Where do you come from?	I _come_ from Scotland, from Dundee.
2	Do you live in Dundee?	No, I _don't_ . I _____ and _____ in London.
3	Do you live with friends?	Yes, I _do_ . I _____ with two friends
4	Where do you work?	I _____ in an Italian restaurant.
5	Do you like Italian food?	Yes, I _____ . I _____ it a lot.
6	Do you drink Italian wine?	Yes, I _____ . I _____ wine but I _____ drink beer. I _____ like it.
7	Do you like your job?	No, I _____ . I want to be _____ _____ .
8	Do you speak Italian?	No, I _____ . I _____ Spanish and French but I _____ speak Italian.

T 5.8 Listen again and check. Practise the questions.

3 Ask and answer the questions with a partner. Give *true* answers about *you*.

GRAMMAR SPOT

a or an?

a small flat   **an** actor   **a** waiter   **an** Italian restaurant

Write *a* or *an*.

___ ice-cream   ___ orange   ___ student   ___ American car   ___ computer

▶▶ **Grammar Reference 5.2 p125**

Vocabulary

4 Match a verb in **A** with a line in **B**.

A	B
have	Italian food
live	sports
work	in a flat
come	two brothers
eat	in a bank
drink	from Japan
play	to be a millionaire
speak	beer
want	Spanish

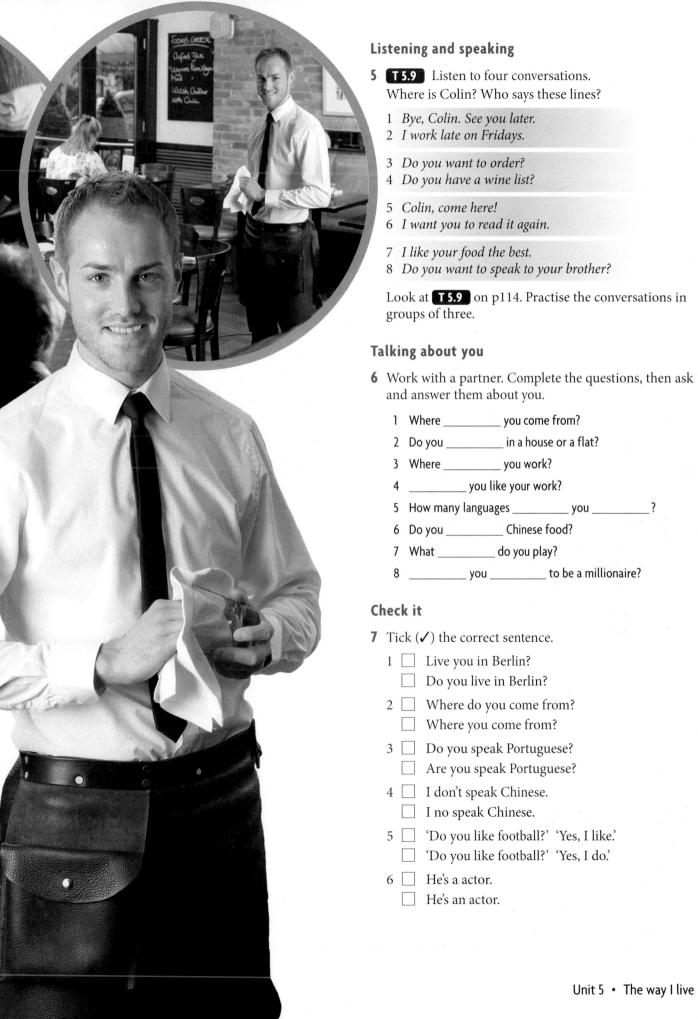

Listening and speaking

5 **T 5.9** Listen to four conversations. Where is Colin? Who says these lines?

1 *Bye, Colin. See you later.*
2 *I work late on Fridays.*

3 *Do you want to order?*
4 *Do you have a wine list?*

5 *Colin, come here!*
6 *I want you to read it again.*

7 *I like your food the best.*
8 *Do you want to speak to your brother?*

Look at **T 5.9** on p114. Practise the conversations in groups of three.

Talking about you

6 Work with a partner. Complete the questions, then ask and answer them about you.

1 Where _____ you come from?
2 Do you _____ in a house or a flat?
3 Where _____ you work?
4 _____ you like your work?
5 How many languages _____ you _____ ?
6 Do you _____ Chinese food?
7 What _____ do you play?
8 _____ you _____ to be a millionaire?

Check it

7 Tick (✓) the correct sentence.

1 ☐ Live you in Berlin?
  ☐ Do you live in Berlin?

2 ☐ Where do you come from?
  ☐ Where you come from?

3 ☐ Do you speak Portuguese?
  ☐ Are you speak Portuguese?

4 ☐ I don't speak Chinese.
  ☐ I no speak Chinese.

5 ☐ 'Do you like football?' 'Yes, I like.'
  ☐ 'Do you like football?' 'Yes, I do.'

6 ☐ He's a actor.
  ☐ He's an actor.

VOCABULARY AND PRONUNCIATION
Languages and nationalities

1 Match the countries and nationalities.

England	Japanese
Germany	French
Italy	English
Mexico	American
Brazil	Chinese
Japan	Italian
Portugal	Brazilian
China	Mexican
France	German
the United States	Portuguese
Spain	Spanish

T 5.10 Listen and repeat.

2 What nationality are the people in the pictures, do you think?

> I think they're Italian.

> Well, I think they're Spanish.

3 Match the countries and the languages to make true sentences.

> In Brazil they speak Portuguese.

Brazil	German
Canada	Italian
France	Japanese
Germany	Portuguese
Italy	Spanish
Japan	English
Mexico	French
Egypt	Arabic
Spain	
Switzerland	

T 5.11 Listen and check.

4 Ask and answer questions with a partner.

> What language do they speak in Brazil?

> Portuguese.

Adjective + noun

5 What is it? Where's it from?

1 It's an _American_ car.

2 It's _____ beer.

3 They're _____ oranges.

6 It's an _____ dictionary.

4 It's a _____ camera.

8 It's _____ coffee.

5 It's _____ food.

7 It's an _____ bag.

9 It's _____ wine.

T 5.12 Listen and check. Practise the sentences.

6 Write sentences about you. Use the verbs *have*, *eat*, and *drink*.

I drink French wine, but I don't drink German beer.

7 Write questions. Ask and answer with a partner.

Do you have an American car?

Yes, I do.

No, I don't. I have a German car.

Do you drink German beer?

Yes, I do.

No, I don't. I don't drink beer. I don't like it.

GRAMMAR SPOT

1 Adjectives come before the noun.

a **Japanese** camera
French wine NOT ~~wine French~~

2 We don't add *-s* to the adjective.

Spanish oranges NOT Spanish~~es~~ oranges
blue jeans NOT blue~~s~~ jeans

▶▶ Grammar Reference 5.3 p125

LISTENING AND SPEAKING
At a party

1 Flavia and Terry are at a party in London.
T 5.13 Listen to the conversation.
Tick (✓) what Terry says.

1 ☐ I work in London.
   ☐ I don't work in London.

2 ☐ I live in London.
   ☐ I don't live in London.

3 ☐ I'm a doctor.
   ☐ I'm an actor.

4 ☐ You speak English very well.
   ☐ You don't speak English very well.

5 ☐ I like Italy.
   ☐ I love Italy.

6 ☐ I know Naples very well.
   ☐ I don't know Naples.

7 ☐ I like Rome very much.
   ☐ I like Naples very much, too.

8 ☐ I speak French and Italian.
   ☐ I don't speak Italian.

2 Look at **T 5.13** on p115. Practise the conversation with a partner.

Roleplay

3 You are at a party. Work with a partner. What are the questions?

- Hello! What's . . . ?
- Where . . . live?
- . . . you have a house or a flat?
- What . . . job?
- Where . . . work?
- How many languages . . . speak?
- What sports . . . you like?

4 Think of a new identity. Make notes to answer the questions in exercise 3.

5 Stand up! Find out about other people at the party.

James Bond . . .
In Rio, Beijing, and London . . .
Three very big apartments . . .
A spy . . . All over the world . . .
Six – French, . . .
Skiing, . . .

EVERYDAY ENGLISH
How much is it?

1 Count from 1–30 round the class.

2 **T 5.14** Listen and repeat.

10 ten   **20** twenty   **30** thirty   **40** forty   **50** fifty   **60** sixty

70 seventy   **80** eighty   **90** ninety   **100** one hundred

Count to 100 in tens round the class.

3 Work with a partner.

Student A
Write some numbers.
Say them to your partner.

thirty-two . . .
forty-five . . .

Student B
Write the numbers you hear.
32   45   . . .

4 **T 5.15** Read and listen to the prices. Practise them.

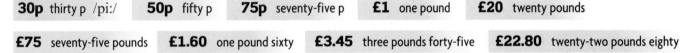

30p thirty p /piː/   **50p** fifty p   **75p** seventy-five p   **£1** one pound   **£20** twenty pounds

£75 seventy-five pounds   **£1.60** one pound sixty   **£3.45** three pounds forty-five   **£22.80** twenty-two pounds eighty

5 Say the prices.

60p   97p   £17   £70   £25   £1.50   £16.80   £40.75   £26.99   €20   €50 $100

T 5.16 Listen and check.

6 **T 5.17** Listen and tick (✓) the prices you hear.

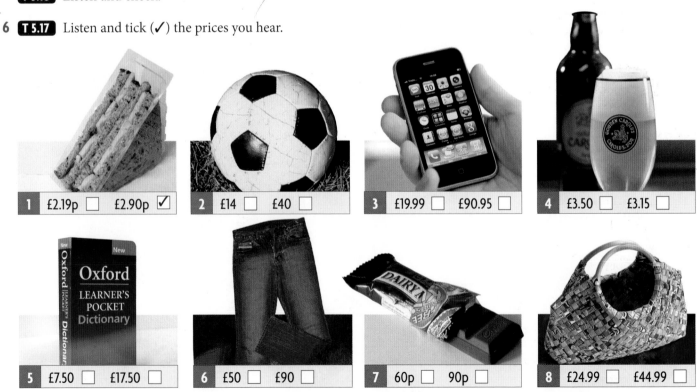

1	£2.19p ☐	£2.90p ✓
2	£14 ☐	£40 ☐
3	£19.99 ☐	£90.95 ☐
4	£3.50 ☐	£3.15 ☐
5	£7.50 ☐	£17.50 ☐
6	£50 ☐	£90 ☐
7	60p ☐	90p ☐
8	£24.99 ☐	£44.99 ☐

7 Ask and answer questions about the pictures with a partner.

How much is the cheese sandwich?   £2.90

6 Every day

The time • Present Simple – *he/she* • *always/sometimes/never*
Words that go together • Days of the week

1 **T 6.1** Listen and repeat. Write the times.

1 It's nine o'clock. **2** It's nine thirty. **3** It's nine forty-five. **4** It's ten o'clock. **5** It's ten fifteen.

6 **7** **8** **9** **10**

2 **T 6.2** Listen to the conversation.

A What time is it, please?
B It's nine o'clock.
A Thank you very much.

Work with a partner. Ask and answer questions about the time.

1

2

3

4

5

WHAT TIME DO YOU GET UP?
Present Simple – *I / you*

1 **T 6.3** Listen to Kim talking about her schooldays. Circle the times.

1 I get up at 7.00 / 7.45

2 I have breakfast at 7.30 / 8.00

3 I go to school at 8.20 / 8.30

4 I have lunch at 12.15 / 12.45

5 I leave school at 3.30 / 4.15

6 I get home at 4.30 / 4.45

7 I go to bed at 11.00 / 11.30

T 6.3 Listen again. Practise the sentences.

2 Work with a partner. Talk about your day.

I get up at 7.30. I have breakfast at . . .

3 **T 6.4** Listen and repeat the questions.

What time **do** you **get up**?
What time **do** you **have** breakfast?

4 Work with another partner.
Ask and answer questions about your day.

What time do you go to work?

I go to work at 8.15.

ELLIOT'S DAY

Present Simple – *he/she*
always/sometimes/never

1 Read about Elliot Maddox and look at the pictures. Are his days busy?

2 Read the sentences about his day. Write the times.

1 He gets up at _six o'clock_ and he has a shower.
2 He has breakfast at _____ .
3 He leaves home at _____ and he goes to work by taxi.
4 He has lunch (a Coca-Cola and a sandwich) in his office at _____ .
5 He always works late. He leaves work at _____ in the evening.
6 He sometimes buys a pizza and eats it at home. He gets home at _____ .
7 He never goes out in the evening. He works at his computer until _____ .
8 He always goes to bed at _____ . He watches television in bed.

T 6.5 Listen and check.

GRAMMAR SPOT

1 Underline the verbs in sentences 1–8.

gets up   has

What's the last letter?

T 6.6 Listen and repeat.

2 Look at the adverbs.

100% ——	50% ——	0%
always	sometimes	never

Find *always*, *sometimes* and *never* in 1–8.

T 6.7 Listen and repeat.

▶▶ Grammar reference 6.1–6.3 p125

Pronunciation

3 **T 6.8** Listen to the pronunciation of *-s* at the end of the verbs. Practise the verbs.

/s/	/z/		/ɪz/
gets up	lives	leaves	watches
works	has	buys	
eats	goes	does	

A DAY IN THE LIFE OF ELLIOT MADDOX

1 6:00 AM

2 6:45 AM

4 1:00 PM

6 9:15 PM

7 9:30 PM – 11:30PM

ELLIOT lives in New York. He's 22, and a computer millionaire. He's the director of netstore24-7.com, a 24-hour shopping site on the Internet. This is a typical day for him.

3

7:15 AM

5

8:00 PM

8

11:45 PM

Questions and negatives

4 Read the questions. Complete the answers.

1 What time **does** he **get up**?
  He _____ at 6.00.

2 When **does** he **go** to bed?
  He _____ to bed at 11.45.

3 **Does** he **go** to work by taxi?
  _____, he **does**.

4 **Does** he **have** lunch in a restaurant?
  _____, he **doesn't**.

5 **Does** he **go out** in the evening?
  No, he _____ .

T 6.9 Listen and check. Practise the questions and answers.

> **GRAMMAR SPOT**
>
> | | |
> |---|---|
> | **Positive** | He **gets up** at 6.00.
 He **has** breakfast at 6.45. |
> | **Negative** | He **doesn't have** lunch.
 He **doesn't go** to bed late.   **doesn't** = does not |
> | **Question** | What time **does** he **have** breakfast?
 Does he **work** late?   Yes, he **does**./No, he **doesn't**. |
>
> ▶▶ **Grammar reference 6.4 p125**

5 Work with a partner. Ask and answer questions about Elliot's day.

1 When/leave home?
2 Does/go to work by bus?
3 Where/have lunch?
4 Does/usually work late?
5 Does/eat in a restaurant?
6 What/do in the evening?

> *When does he leave home?*
>
> *He leaves home at . . .*

T 6.10 Listen and check.

6 Write negative sentences.

1 live/London   *He doesn't live in London.*
2 drive to work   4 have a lot of friends
3 work in a bank   5 go to bed late

7 Complete the chart in the Present Simple.

	Positive	Negative	Question
I	work		Do I work?
You			
He/She	works		Does she work?
We		don't work	
They			

PRACTICE
Lois's day

1 Elliot Maddox has a sister, Lois. Her day is different. Look at the pictures. What does she do?

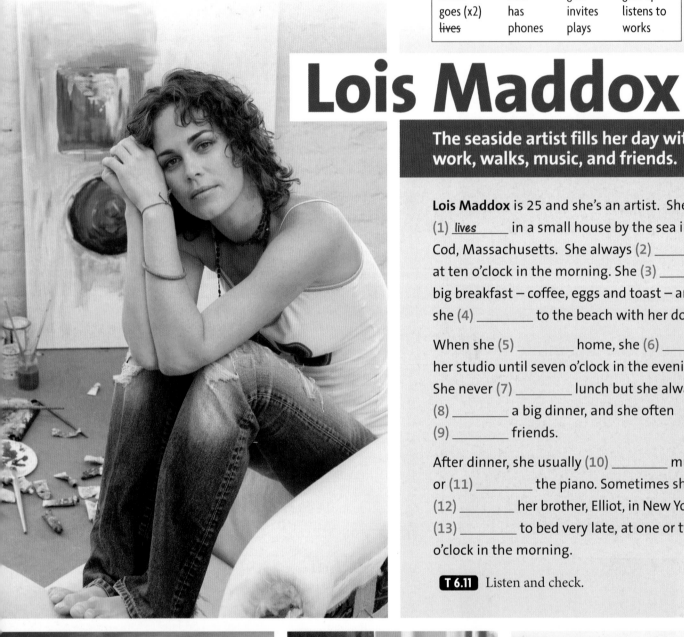

2 Read and complete the text with the verbs.

cooks	eats	gets	gets up
goes (x2)	has	invites	listens to
~~lives~~	phones	plays	works

Lois Maddox

The seaside artist fills her day with work, walks, music, and friends.

Lois Maddox is 25 and she's an artist. She
(1) _lives_____ in a small house by the sea in Cape
Cod, Massachusetts. She always (2) _____ late,
at ten o'clock in the morning. She (3) _____ a
big breakfast – coffee, eggs and toast – and then
she (4) _____ to the beach with her dog.

When she (5) _____ home, she (6) _____ in
her studio until seven o'clock in the evening.
She never (7) _____ lunch but she always
(8) _____ a big dinner, and she often
(9) _____ friends.

After dinner, she usually (10) _____ music
or (11) _____ the piano. Sometimes she
(12) _____ her brother, Elliot, in New York. She
(13) _____ to bed very late, at one or two
o'clock in the morning.

T 6.11 Listen and check.

3 Are these sentences about Lois or Elliot? Write *He* or *She*.

1 _He_'s a millionaire.
2 _____'s an artist.
3 _____ lives by the sea.
4 _____ gets up very early.
5 _____ doesn't eat lunch.
6 _____ doesn't cook.
7 _____ cooks for friends.
8 _____ loves computers.

Practise the sentences.

4 **T 6.12** Listen and complete the phone conversation between Lois and Elliot.

Lois Hi Elliot, how are you?

Elliot I'm _fine____, thanks. Busy as usual.

L Oh, you're _____ busy. You and your computers!

E I know, but I _____ my work.

L I love my work, _____, but I relax _____.

E Huh! I don't know about that. You paint all day!

L Yes, but I stop in the _____. You _____ stop!

E That's not true. Hey Lois, how's your friend Nancy?

L Nancy? She's OK. You know, Elliot, Nancy _____ you. She often _____ about you.

E Mm, I like Nancy, too.

L Well, come and _____ me soon. I want to cook for you and Nancy.

E Good idea! What about next _____? Next Sunday?

L Yes, great! I _____ invite Nancy at the weekend.

E Great. See you _____ Sunday. Have a good week!

T 6.12 Listen again and check. Practise the conversation with a partner.

Negatives and pronunciation

5 Correct the sentences about Lois and Elliot.

1 She lives in a flat.
   She doesn't live in a flat! She lives in a house!
2 He gets up at ten o'clock.
   _____
3 She's a businesswoman.
   _____
4 He goes to work by bus.
   _____
5 She watches television in the evening.
   _____

T 6.13 Listen and check. Notice the sentence stress. Practise with a partner.

Talking about you

6 Work with a partner. Write the names of two people in your family. Ask and answer questions about them.

Sonya

> Who's she?
> She's my aunt.

Jim

> Who's he?
> He's my dad.

- Who is ...?
- How old is ...?
- What's ... job?
- Where does ... live?
- Where does ... work?
- What time does she/he ...?
- Does she/he have ...?

Check it

7 Complete the questions and answers with *do*, *don't*, *does*, or *doesn't*.

1 '_____ you like ice-cream?'
   'Yes, I _____.'
2 '_____ she work in London?'
   'Yes, she _____.'
3 'Where _____ he work?'
   'In a bank.'
4 '_____ you go to work by bus?'
   'No, I _____.'
5 '_____ she go to bed early?'
   'No, she _____.'
6 '_____ they have a dog?'
   'Yes, they _____.'
7 '_____ he speak German?'
   'No, he _____.'
8 '_____ they live in the US?'
   'No, they _____.'

VOCABULARY AND SPEAKING
Words that go together

1 Match a verb in **A** with words in **B**.
T 6.14 Listen and check.

A	B
get up	dinner
go	early
listen to	TV
watch	in an office
cook	music
work	to bed late

A	B
go	in restaurants
drink	the piano
eat	coffee
have	shopping
play	at home
stay	a shower

2 **T 6.15** Look at the questionnaire. Listen and repeat the questions.

lifestyle *questionnaire*

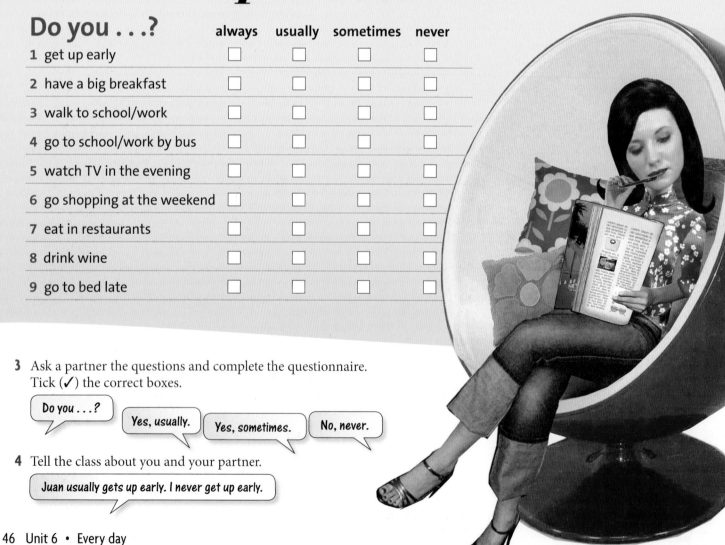

Do you . . . ?

	always	usually	sometimes	never
1 get up early	☐	☐	☐	☐
2 have a big breakfast	☐	☐	☐	☐
3 walk to school/work	☐	☐	☐	☐
4 go to school/work by bus	☐	☐	☐	☐
5 watch TV in the evening	☐	☐	☐	☐
6 go shopping at the weekend	☐	☐	☐	☐
7 eat in restaurants	☐	☐	☐	☐
8 drink wine	☐	☐	☐	☐
9 go to bed late	☐	☐	☐	☐

3 Ask a partner the questions and complete the questionnaire.
Tick (✓) the correct boxes.

Do you . . . ?

Yes, usually.   Yes, sometimes.   No, never.

4 Tell the class about you and your partner.

Juan usually gets up early. I never get up early.

EVERYDAY ENGLISH

Days of the week

1 **T 6.16** Listen and write the days in the correct order on the calendar.

> Wednesday ~~Monday~~ Friday Tuesday
> Thursday Sunday Saturday

T 6.16 Listen again and repeat.

2 Work with a partner. Ask and answer the questions.
1 What day is it today?
2 What day is it tomorrow?
3 What days do you go to school/work?
4 What days are the weekend?
5 What days do you like?
6 What days don't you like?

3 Write the correct preposition in the boxes.

on in at

	nine o'clock
	ten thirty
	twelve fifteen
	the weekend

	Sunday
	Monday
	Saturday evening
	Thursday morning
	Friday afternoon

	the morning
	the afternoon
	the evening

4 Write the correct preposition. Then ask and answer the questions with your partner.

> **Do you have English lessons . . . ?**
>
> 1 __at__ nine o'clock

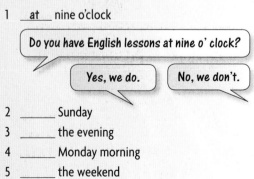

Do you have English lessons at nine o' clock?

Yes, we do.   No, we don't.

> 2 _____ Sunday
> 3 _____ the evening
> 4 _____ Monday morning
> 5 _____ the weekend

When do *you* have English lessons?   We have English lessons . . .

Talking about you

5 Complete the questions. Ask and answer them with your partner.

> **Do you . . . ?**
> • have a shower _____ the morning/evening
> • get up early _____ Sunday morning
> • go to work/school _____ Saturday
> • eat in restaurants _____ the weekend
> • watch TV _____ the afternoon
> • stay at home _____ Friday evening

7 My favourites

Question words • *me/him/us/them* • *this/that*
Adjectives • *Can I …?*

STARTER

1 What is your favourite …?

> food   drink   sport   song
> TV programme   day of the week   town or city

2 Ask and answer with a partner.

> What's your favourite food?

> Pizza. I love it.

I LOVE IT!

Question words – *me/him/us/them*

1 Who is Gina Macy? Look at the pictures.

2 [T 7.1] Read and listen to Gina's website. What is her favourite …?
• city • day • designer • food

3 Find the question word that completes the questions to Gina.

1 **Where** do you live?
2 _____ are you married to?
3 _____ does your husband do?
4 _____ are you in Sydney again?
5 _____ are the kids in the photos?
6 _____ old are they?
7 _____ do your daughters have Swedish names? Because …
8 _____ shows do you do every year?
9 _____ do you work so hard? Because …
10 _____ do you do in your free time?

4 Ask and answer the questions with a partner.

> Where do you live?

> I live in France, in Paris.

[T 7.2] Listen and compare.

Gina Macy

Gina Macy, fashion model, answers your questions.

1 GERRY from TEXAS

You're American, but you don't live in the US. So where do you live?

GINA Hi Gerry! I live in France, in Paris. A lot of my work is here. Paris is my favourite city. I love it here.

2 DENG from SINGAPORE

I know you are divorced. Who are you married to now? What does your husband do?

GINA I'm married to a Frenchman now, Julien Caribe. He's a photographer. I love him very much and he loves me, so we're very happy.

3 MIRIAM from SYDNEY

I watch all your fashion shows. I love your clothes. Do you choose them? Who is your favourite designer? When are you in Sydney again?

GINA Thank you Miriam. No, we don't choose our clothes, the fashion house chooses them for us. Chanel is my favourite designer. We're in Sydney next October.

4 SILVIO from ROME

I love your website. Who are the kids in the photos? How old are they?

GINA The girls are my daughters Freja, she's six, and Frida, she's four. The baby is our son, Pierre-Louis, he's ten months old. I adore them all.

5 INGRID from STOCKHOLM

Why do your daughters have Swedish names?

GINA Because their father is Swedish. He is Lars Lonnkvist the film director. It's sad, but he never visits us. He doesn't often see his beautiful daughters.

6 JULIE from OXFORD

You do a lot of fashion shows. How many shows do you do every year? Why do you work so hard? What do you and Julien do in your free time?

GINA Julie, I work hard because I love my work. I do about eight big shows a year. But I love my family too. Friday is our favourite day, we all go to the best pizza restaurant in Paris. Pizza's my favourite food!

5 Complete the sentences with the words from Gina's website.

1 Paris is __my__ favourite city. I love __it__ here.

2 I love _____ very much and he loves _____.

3 We don't choose _____ clothes. The fashion house chooses _____ for _____.

4 The girls are _____ daughters and the boy is _____ son. I adore _____ all.

5 _____ father is Swedish. It's sad, but he never visits _____.

6 Friday is _____ favourite day.

6 Correct the information about Gina.

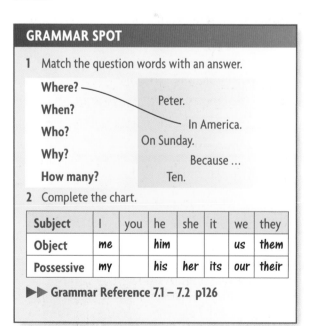

ginamacy.com > Profile

            model

Gina is a fashion ~~photographer~~. New York is her favourite city. She loves it there. Next October she's in Singapore for a fashion show. She's now married to an American. They have a baby daughter. Saturday is their favourite day.

T 7.3 Listen and check. Read it aloud.

GRAMMAR SPOT

1 Match the question words with an answer.

Where? ———   Peter.

When?   → In America.

Who?   On Sunday.

Why?   Because …

How many?   Ten.

2 Complete the chart.

Subject	I	you	he	she	it	we	they
Object	me		him			us	them
Possessive	my		his	her	its	our	their

▶▶ Grammar Reference 7.1 – 7.2 p126

THIS IS MY FAVOURITE ...

this and *that*

1 Look at the pictures. Complete the conversations with *this* or *that*.

1

A __This__ is my favourite family photo.
B Ah, yes. You all look very happy!

2

C Who's __that__ ?
D The guy in the hat? That's the boss!

3

E What's _____ ?
F It's my new MP3 player.
E Wow! It's great!

4

G How much is _____ ?
H £9.50.
G I'll have it, please.

5

I How much is _____ ?
J It's £500.
I I love it. It's fantastic!

6

K Is _____ your phone?
L Yes, it is. Thanks.

7

M I like _____ coat.
N The blue one?
M No, the red one!

8

O I like _____ wine.
P Where's it from?
O Chile. It's delicious.

9

Q _____ is for you.
R A present? For me? Why?
Q Because I love you!

T 7.4 Listen and check.

▶▶ **Grammar Reference 7.3 p126**

2 Test the other students! Ask them questions about things in your classroom.

What's this in English?

It's a newspaper.

What's that in English?

It's a door.

PRACTICE

I like them!

1 Complete the sentences with *it, you, them* …

1 'Do you like ice-cream?'
  'Yes, I love __it__.'

2 'Do you like dogs?'
  'No, I hate _____.'

3 'Do you like me?'
  'Of course I like _____!'

4 'Does your teacher teach you French?'
  'No, she teaches _____ English.'

5 'Do you like your teacher?'
  'We like _____ very much.'

T 7.5 Listen and check.

What do you like?

2 Ask and answer questions with a partner. Ask about …

| football | cats | television | ice-cream | chips | dogs |
| mobile phones | Google | pop music | your neighbours |

Do you like football?

Yes, I love it!

No! I hate it!

Do you like cats?

Oh yes! I adore them.

Questions and answers

3 Work with a partner. Ask and answer the questions.

1 Why/you live in London?   __Why do you live in London?__   (… like …)   __Because I like it.__

2 Why/Annie want to marry Peter?   _____   (… love …)   _____

3 Why/you eat so much chocolate?   _____   (… adore …)   _____

4 Why/Dan always sit next to Maria?   _____   (… like …)   _____

5 Why/you/not watch football?   _____   (… hate …)   _____

6 Why/you/not eat carrots?   _____   (… hate …)   _____

4 Match the questions and answers.

1 How do you come to school?   a They start at nine o'clock.
2 What do you have for breakfast?   b In an office in the centre of town.
3 Who's your favourite band?   c By bus.
4 Where does your father work?   d Not a lot. About £2.
5 Why do you want to learn English?   e I don't have a favourite. I like a lot.
6 How much money do you have on you?   f Three.
7 What time do lessons start at your school? g Because it's an international language.
8 How many languages does your teacher speak? h Toast and coffee.

T 7.6 Listen and check. Practise the questions.

Work with a partner. Ask and answer the questions about you.

Check it

5 Tick (✓) the correct sentence.

1 ☐ What do you do at the weekend?
  ☐ Where do you do at the weekend?

2 ☐ Who is your boyfriend?
  ☐ When is your boyfriend?

3 ☐ How many money do you have?
  ☐ How much money do you have?

4 ☐ I don't drink beer. I don't like.
  ☐ I don't drink beer. I don't like it.

5 ☐ Our teacher gives us a lot of homework.
  ☐ Our teacher gives we a lot of homework.

6 ☐ She loves me and I love her.
  ☐ She loves my and I love she.

VOCABULARY

Adjectives

1 Write the words.

1 This pizza is _d e l i c i o u s_. (L E S I C I U D O)
2 Your sister is really _ _ _ _ _. (C E N I)
3 Our house is _ _ _ _ _ _ _. (V O L E Y L)
4 I'm really _ _ _ _ _ today. (A P Y H P)
5 Our English lessons are _ _ _ _ _ _ _ _ _ _ _ _. (N T I R S E G N T I E)
6 Paris is a _ _ _ _ _ _ _ _ _ city. (E T F L B A U I U)
7 Rain again! The weather is _ _ _ _ _ _ _ _! (R E B T R I L E)
8 Ugh! This coffee is _ _ _ _ _ _! (F W A U L)

2 Match the words and pictures.

| new/old | expensive/cheap | ~~big/small~~ | hot/cold | right/wrong | black/white |

1 It's big. / It's small.

4 _____ / _____

2 _____ / _____

5 _____ / _____

3 _____ / _____

6 _____ / _____

3 **T 7.7** Listen and complete the conversations.

1 **A** It's so _hot_ today, isn't it?
  B I know. It's _____ degrees!

2 **C** Hey! I like your _____ shoes!
  D Thank you! They're really nice, aren't they?
  C They're _____!

3 **E** I live in a very _____ flat.
  F How many bedrooms do you have?
  E Only _____!

4 **G** How _____ is that coat?
  H £150.
  G Wow! That's too _____ for me.

5 **I** Your name's Peter, isn't it?
  J Yes, that's _____.
  I _____ to meet you, Peter.

Practise the conversations with a partner.

READING AND WRITING
A postcard from San Francisco

1 **T 7.8** Look at the postcard. Read and listen.

Dear Allen,

We're on holiday in San Francisco this week. Our hotel is very nice – old but comfortable. The people are very friendly, but it isn't easy to understand them. They speak so fast!

The food is delicious, especially the seafood, and the cafés and restaurants are wonderful!

San Francisco is beautiful. It's a big city, with a lot of new buildings, and it isn't expensive. The shops are great, and the Golden Gate Bridge is amazing!

The weather is awful – rain and fog. It's cold and wet, but we're very happy!

See you next week.

Love

Ruben and Pasha (your Mexican students!)

Allen Birch
the English School
120 Magazine Rd.
Boston, MA
02148

2 Answer the questions.
1 Who is the postcard from?
2 Where are they?
3 Why are they in San Francisco?
4 Is their holiday good?
5 What isn't so good?

3 What adjectives do Ruben and Pasha use?

	Adjectives
their hotel	nice, old, comfortable
the people	
the food	
the cafés and restaurants	
San Francisco	
the shops	
the Golden Gate Bridge	
the weather	

Writing

4 Write a postcard to a friend.

Dear ...

We're on holiday in ... and it's very ...
Our hotel is ...
The people are ...
The food is ...
The weather is ..., and ... we go ...

See you soon.
Love ...

EVERYDAY ENGLISH

Can I . . . ?

1 Write a number **1–5** (place) and a letter **a–e** (activity) for each picture.

PLACES	ACTIVITIES
1 a chemist	a have a coffee
~~2~~ a railway station	b buy some aspirin
3 a post office	c post letters
4 a clothes shop	~~d~~ catch a train
5 a café	e try on a jumper

2 d

Iveta in town

2 **T 7.9** Listen to Iveta. She is in different places in town. Where is she in the conversations? What does she want?

Where is she?	What does she want?
1 at the railway station	a return ticket to Oxford
2	
3	
4	
5	

3 Complete the conversations with a partner.

1 IN A RAILWAY STATION

I Can I have a return _____ to Oxford, please?
A Sure.
I How much _____ _____?
A Twenty-two _____ fifty, please.
I Can I _____ by _____ card?
A No problem. Put your card in the machine.
  And enter your PIN number, please.

2 IN A CLOTHES SHOP

I Hello. Can I _____ _____ this jumper, please?
B _____ _____ . The changing rooms are over there.

3 IN A POST OFFICE

I _____ _____ post these letters to the Czech Republic, _____ ?
C Sure. Put them on the scales. That's £1.68.
I Thank you. _____ _____ is a stamp for a postcard to the United States?
C _____ -two p.
I Can I have _____ , please?

4 IN A CAFÉ

D Yes, please!
I Can I have _____ _____ , please? A latte.
D Large or small?
I _____ _____ . To take away.
D Sure. Anything to eat?
I No, _____ _____ . Just a coffee.
D Thanks _____ _____ .

5 IN A CHEMIST'S

E Next, please!
I Hello. Can I have _____ _____ , please?
E Twelve or twenty-four?
I _____ ?
E Do you want a packet of twelve aspirin or twenty-four?
I Oh, twelve's _____ , thanks.

T 7.10 Listen and check. Practise the conversations.

Roleplay

4 Work with a partner. Make more conversations with different information.

- a return/single ticket to Manchester/Bristol
- this jacket/this T-shirt
- this parcel to Italy/this letter to Russia
- a cheese and salad sandwich/an ice-cream
- shampoo/toothpaste

Where I live

Rooms and furniture • *There is / are* • Prepositions • Directions

1 Do you live in a house or a flat? Do you have a garden or a balcony? Tell the class.

> I live in a flat.

> We don't have a garden but we have a big balcony.

2 **T 8.1** Look at the picture. Listen and repeat the rooms of a house.

living room, dining room . . .

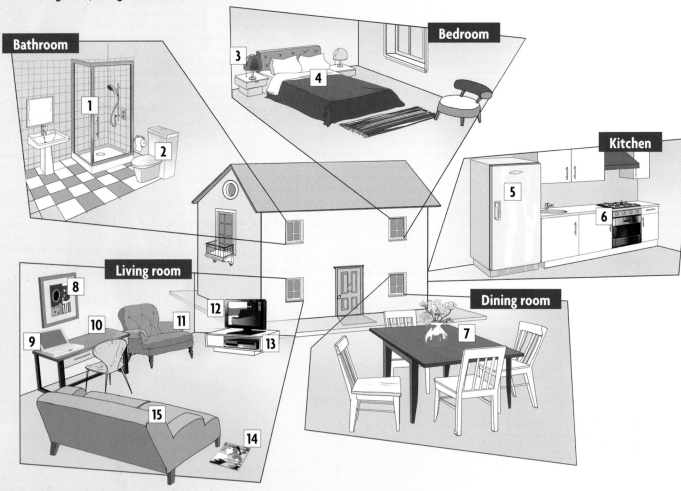

3 Find the things in the house. Write the numbers.

[4] a bed	☐ a TV	☐ a table	☐ a lamp	☐ a DVD player
☐ a cooker	☐ a shower	☐ a fridge	☐ a picture	☐ a laptop
☐ a sofa	☐ a toilet	☐ an armchair	☐ a magazine	☐ a desk

T 8.2 Listen and repeat.

ROBERT'S LIVING ROOM
There is/are . . .

1 **T 8.3** Read and listen to Robert describing his living room. Complete his description.

'My living room isn't very big, but I think it's great. There's an old sofa, and there are two armchairs. _____ 's a table with a TV and a DVD player on it. _____ also a PlayStation®. I love all the games. There _____ some books, and _____ are a lot of pictures and posters on the walls. _____ _____ two lamps. My room's not very tidy but it's really comfortable.'

2 Talk about Robert's living room.

> There's an old sofa.

> There are two armchairs.

- a sofa
- armchairs
- a DVD player
- a table
- books
- lamps
- posters
- a PlayStation®

3 **T 8.4** Listen and repeat the questions and answers.

Is there a sofa?	✓ Yes, there is.
Is there a desk?	✗ No, there isn't.
Are there any armchairs?	✓ Yes, there are.
Are there any photographs?	✗ No, there aren't.

Practise them with a partner.

GRAMMAR SPOT

Complete the sentences.

Positive	**There's** a sofa.
	_____ _____ two armchairs.
Question	_____ _____ a TV?
	Are there any pictures?
Negative	**There isn't** a computer.
	_____ _____ any photographs.

▶▶ Grammar reference 8.1 – 8.2 p126

4 Ask and answer questions about Robert's living room.

- a TV
- photographs
- a desk
- a telephone
- lamps
- a DVD player
- a PlayStation®
- magazines

> Is there a TV?

> Yes, there is.

> Are there any photographs?

> No, there aren't.

5 Look again at Robert's living room. Is it tidy?

T 8.5 Listen to Robert talking to his mother.

1 What things in his flat does she ask about?
2 What are her questions?
3 When does she want to visit?

Look at **T 8.5** on p117. Practise the conversation with a partner.

6 Work with a partner. Describe your living room.

In my living room there's a ...   There are a lot of ...

ROBERT'S BEDROOM

Prepositions

1 Look at the prepositions.

in	on	under	next to

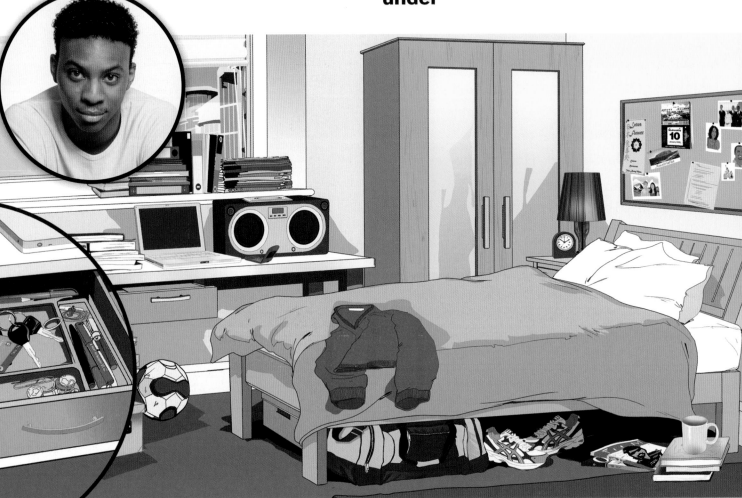

2 Look at Robert's bedroom. Write a preposition from exercise 1.

1 His laptop is __on__ the desk.

2 The CD player is _____ the laptop.

3 There are three books _____ the floor _____ his bed.

4 His car keys are _____ the drawer.

5 There's a football _____ the floor _____ the desk.

6 His trainers are _____ his bag _____ his bed.

T 8.6 Listen and check. Practise the sentences.

3 Ask and answer questions about Robert's things.

> Where's Robert's CD player?
>
> It's on the desk next to the laptop.
>
> Where are his car keys?
>
> They're in the drawer.

Ask about his …

- CD player
- car keys
- sports bag
- pens

- magazines
- credit cards
- jumper
- lamp

- alarm clock
- trainers
- photos
- mug

4 Close your eyes! Ask and answer questions about things in your classroom.

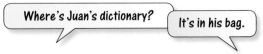

> Where's Juan's dictionary?
>
> It's in his bag.

PRACTICE

Questions and answers

1 Put the words in the correct order to make questions.

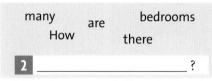
house live Do you
a or in flat a
1 Do you live in a house or a flat ?

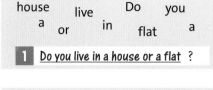
many bedrooms
How are there
2 _____ ?

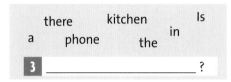
there kitchen Is
a phone the in
3 _____ ?

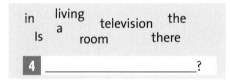
in living the
Is a television
room there
4 _____ ?

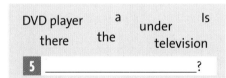
DVD player a Is
there the under television
5 _____ ?

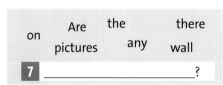
there in Are your
bedroom books
a lot of
6 _____ ?

on Are the there
pictures any wall
7 _____ ?

T 8.7 Listen and check.

2 Work with a partner. Ask and answer the questions about your home.

Two different rooms

3 Work with a partner.

Student A Look at the picture on this page.
Student B Look at the picture on p141.

Your pictures are different. Talk about them to find differences.

In my picture, there's a …

In my picture, there isn't a …

Is there a …?

Yes, there is. / No, there isn't.

4 **T 8.8** Listen to a description of one of the rooms. Which room is it?

Check it

5 Tick (✓) the correct sentence.

1 ☐ Is a sofa in the living room?
  ☐ Is there a sofa in the living room?

2 ☐ There's DVD player on the floor.
  ☐ There's a DVD player on the floor.

3 ☐ Are there a poster on the wall?
  ☐ Are there any posters on the wall?

4 ☐ My keys are in the drawer.
  ☐ My keys are on the drawer.

5 ☐ The lamp is next to the bed.
  ☐ The lamp is next the bed.

READING AND VOCABULARY
Vancouver – the best city in the world

1 Work with a partner. Look at the map and find Vancouver. Is it near the US?

2 Look at the pictures. Find these things.
- mountains
- the sea
- a beach
- a ferry
- a trolley bus
- a train
- a park
- sailing
- fishing

3 Read the text about Vancouver. Write the five paragraph headings in the correct place.

Where is it?

Where to stay

When to go

What to do

How to travel

Where to eat

T 8.9 Listen and check.

4 Answer the questions.
1 Where is Vancouver?
2 When is a good time to visit?
3 Does it rain a lot? When?
4 What do people do … ?
   - in the mountains
   - on the beach
   - in Stanley Park
5 What water sports are there?
6 Why are there so many kinds of restaurants?
7 Are *all* the hotels expensive? How much are they?
8 What is a good way to see the city?

5 Complete the chart with adjectives from the text.

Adjectives	Nouns
busy, cosmopolitan	city
	mountains
	beaches
	shops and restaurants
	the weather
	seafood
	hotels
	trolley buses
	Sky Train

Vancouver, Canada

Vancouver is called the

'best city in the world'.

Why? Is it the spectacular mountains?
The beautiful beaches?
The excellent shops and restaurants?
It's all of this and more!

Where is it?

Vancouver is in south-west Canada, next to the Pacific Ocean, 24 miles from the US border.

It is always a good time to visit Vancouver. The weather is never too cold or too hot. It is warm and sunny in summer, but it rains a lot in autumn and winter.

In spring, go skiing in the mountains in the morning and sunbathe on the beach in the afternoon. In summer, go swimming, sailing or fishing, or go walking in North America's biggest park, Stanley Park. There are excellent shops in Yaletown, and there is also theatre, opera, and music of every sort. Vancouver is the 'City of Festivals'.

Vancouver is a cosmopolitan city so there are French, Italian, Japanese, Indian, Thai, and Chinese restaurants. Vancouver's Chinatown is the second biggest in North America, after San Francisco. There is also a lot of delicious, fresh seafood.

In the busy city centre there are some excellent, expensive hotels. The beautiful Fairmont Hotel is $400 a night, but next to the sea there are a lot of cheap, comfortable hotels from $59 a night.

You don't need a car in Vancouver. There are slow, old trolley buses and there is the fast, modern Sky Train. Take the ferry – it is a great way to see the city.

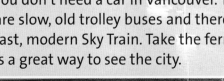

LISTENING AND WRITING
My home town

1 **T 8.10** Listen to Steve. He lives in Vancouver. Tick (✓) the things he talks about.

- ☐ his job
- ☐ sunbathing
- ☐ his apartment
- ☐ his girlfriend
- ☐ Chinatown
- ☐ Italian food
- ☐ the theatre
- ☐ the weather
- ☐ skiing
- ☐ golf
- ☐ cycling
- ☐ Stanley Park

2 **T 8.10** Listen again. Answer the questions.
1 Where does Steve work?
2 Where does he live?
3 Is his apartment big?
4 What is his favourite food?
5 Does he always like the weather?
6 Where does he go with his girlfriend after work?
7 What sports does Steve like?
8 Where does he cycle with his girlfriend?

3 **T 8.11** Listen to four conversations with Steve. Complete the chart.

	What is the conversation about?	Who is Steve talking to?
1		
2		
3		
4		

Look at **T 8.11** on p117. Practise the conversations with a partner.

4 In groups, talk about *your* home town.
- Where do you live?
- What is there in your town?
- What do you do there with your friends?
- Where do you go shopping?
- How do you travel?
- Is it a good place to live?

Writing

5 Write about a town you know.

Where is it?	. . . is a town in . . .
When to visit	The best time to visit is . . .
What to do	Go . . . There are a lot of . . .
Where to eat	There are good restaurants in . . . My favourite restaurant is . . .
Where to stay	. . . is an expensive hotel in . . . . . . is a cheap hotel near/next to . . .
How to travel	The best way to see the town is . . .

EVERYDAY ENGLISH
Directions

1 Find the places on the map.

hotel	bank	chemist's	post office	newsagent's	church	supermarket	park
Internet café	railway station	theatre	sports centre	car park	cinema	pub	

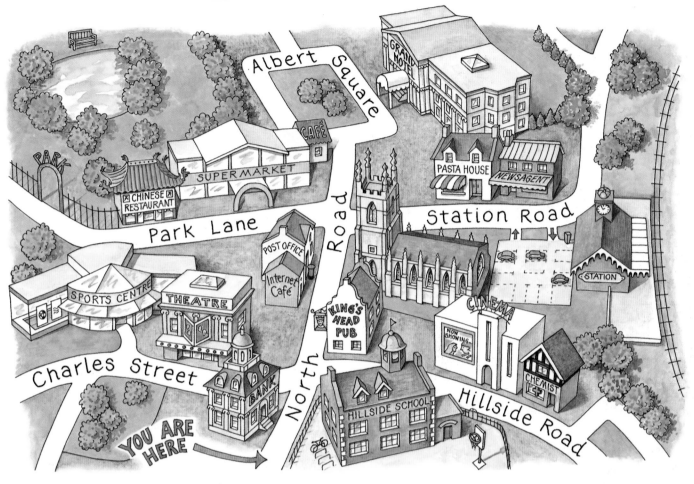

2 What do the signs mean?

turn right	go straight on	turn left

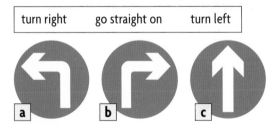

a   b   c

3 **T 8.12** Listen to the directions. Start from YOU ARE HERE on the map. Follow the directions. Where are you?

1 *Go up North Road. Turn left at the bank into Charles Street. It's on the right next to the theatre.*

   <u>at the sports centre</u>

2 _____

3 _____

4 _____

5 _____

Look at **T 8.12** on p118. Practise the directions.

4 Work with a partner. Have similar conversations.

Ask about …

• a cinema
• a post office
• a newsagent's
• a supermarket
• a car park
• a café

> **Excuse me! Is there a . . . near here?**
>
> **Yes. Go down . . .**

5 With your partner, ask for and give directions to places in your town.

> **How do I get to the bus station?**
>
> **Go out of the school, turn right . . .**
>
> **Is it far?**
>
> **About ten minutes.**

9 Times past

Saying years • *was/were born* • Past Simple – irregular verbs • *have/do/go* •
When's your birthday?

STARTER

1 **T 9.1** Listen and <u>underline</u> the years you hear. Say them.

1 <u>1996</u> / 1986   **2** 1916 / 1960   **3** 2010 / 2002   **4** 1699 / 1799   **5** 1840 / 1945   **6** 2005 / 2015

2 **T 9.2** Listen and repeat.

1840 eighteen forty   **1996** nineteen ninety-six   **2005** two thousand and five   **2010** two thousand and ten / twenty ten

3 What year is it now? What year was it last year? What year is it next year?

WHEN WAS SHE BORN?
was/were born

1 Look at the photos. Do you know the people? When were they born?
T 9.3 Listen and write the years.

Jane Austen (17** – 1817)

Jane Austen, the English writer, was born
in _____ in Hampshire in the south of England.

Luciano Pavarotti (19** – 2007)

Luciano Pavarotti, the Italian opera singer, was
born in _____ in Modena in the north of Italy.

2 **T 9.4** Listen and repeat.

She was a writer. She was born in _____ .

He was an opera singer. He was born in _____.

3 Ask and answer questions with other students.

> How old are you?

> I'm 18/21 … I was born in 19 …

4 [**T 9.5**] Listen to the questions and answers. Practise them.

When **were** you born? — I was born in 1994.
When **was** he born? — He was born in 1978.
When **was** she born? — She was born in 1991.
When **were** they born? — They were born in 2001.

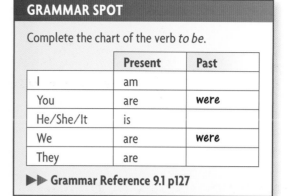

GRAMMAR SPOT

Complete the chart of the verb *to be*.

	Present	Past
I	am	
You	are	**were**
He/She/It	is	
We	are	**were**
They	are	

▶▶ **Grammar Reference 9.1 p127**

5 [**T 9.6**] This is Magalie Dromard. Listen to her talking about her family. Write when the people were born.

MAGALIE DROMARD

MY FAMILY

Magalie	1994
Tristan	_____
Cecilia	_____
Matt	_____
André	_____
Ella	_____
Edith	_____

Work with a partner. Ask and answer questions about Magalie's family.

> Who's Tristan?

> He's Magalie's brother.

> When was he born?

> In 1985.

> Who are André and Ella?

> They're her …

> When were they … ?

6 Who is your grandmother/grandfather/aunt/uncle …?

Write the names of some people in your family. Ask and answer questions about them.

> Ernest   Mary

A Who's Ernest?
B He's my uncle.

A When was he born?
B I'm not sure. I think about 1935.

Ernest

Mary

7 Tell the class about your partner's family.

Peter's uncle was born in 1956.
His mother was born in 1962.

PRACTICE

Who were they?

1 Who are the people in the photographs?
Match the people 1–8 and the jobs in the box.

☐ singer	☐ writer	☐ politician
☐ musician	☐ artist	☐ racing driver
☐ actor	☐ princess	

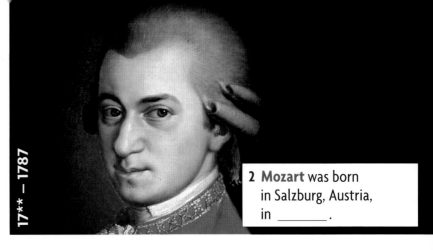

17** – 1787

2 Mozart was born in Salzburg, Austria, in _____.

15** – 1616

1 Shakespeare was born in __1564__, in Stratford-upon-Avon, England.

19** – 1997

3 Diana Spencer was born in Sandringham, England, in _____.

2 **T 9.7** Listen and write when they were born.

3 **T 9.8** Listen to the questions and answers. Practise them.

Who was Shakespeare?	He was a writer.
Where was he born?	In England.
When was he born?	In 1564.

Work with a partner. Ask and answer the questions about the other people.

Who was Andy Warhol?   He was an . . .

19** – 1987

4 Andy Warhol was born in _____, in Pittsburgh, in the US.

19** – 2009

5 Michael Jackson was born in _____, in Indiana, in the US.

6 Benazir Bhutto was born in Karachi, Pakistan, in _____ .

19** – 2007

7 Marilyn Monroe was born in _____ , in Los Angeles, in the US.

19** – 1962

8 Ayrton Senna was born in São Paulo, Brazil, in _____ .

19** – 1994

Negatives and pronunciation

4 **T 9.9** Listen and repeat.

Shakespeare was an artist.
No, he wasn't. He was a writer.

Shakespeare and Diana were Irish.
No, they weren't. They were English.

5 Write the correct information.

1 Ayrton Senna was an actor.
   No, he _wasn't_ ! _He was a racing driver_ !
2 Jane Austen was a princess.
   No, she _____ ! _____ !
3 Marilyn Monroe and Michael Jackson were Italian.
   No, they _____ ! _____ !
4 Mozart was a scientist.
   No, he _____ ! _____ !
5 Luciano Pavarotti and Michael Jackson were politicians.
   No, they _____ ! _____ !
6 Benazir Bhutto was a writer.
   No, she _____ ! _____ !

T 9.10 Listen and check. Practise the sentences.

Today and yesterday

6 What is true for you? Tell a partner.

Today is . . . Yesterday was . . .	Monday / Tuesday / Wednesday . . .
Today I'm . . . Yesterday I was . . .	at school / at home / at work . . .
Today the weather is . . . Yesterday the weather was . . .	hot / cold / wet / lovely / horrible . . .
Today my parents are . . . Yesterday my parents were . . .	at work / at home . . .

Check it

7 Complete the sentences with *was*, *wasn't*, *were*, or *weren't*.

1 Where _was_ your mother born?
2 When _____ your parents born?
3 No, my parents _____ both born in 1951. My father _____ born in 1951, and my mother _____ born in 1953.
4 I _____ on holiday in New York in 2008.
5 '_____ he at home yesterday?' 'No, he _____'
6 '_____ you at work yesterday?' 'Yes, we _____.'
7 '_____ they at school yesterday morning?' 'No, they _____.'

READING AND SPEAKING
Past Simple – irregular verbs

1 Match the present and the past forms of the verbs.
Look at the Irregular verbs list on p142.

Present	Past
go	saw
come	went
have	said
be	made
make	came
see	had
buy	found
say	bought /bɔːt/
find	was

T 9.11 Listen and check. Practise the verbs.

▶▶ **Grammar Reference 9.2 p127**

2 Look at the pictures. They tell a true story.
Match the sentences and pictures.

a The painting is now for sale in an art gallery in Canada.

b An American lady went shopping and bought a painting for $5 from a charity shop.

c A rich businessman was happy to pay $9 million, but Teri said 'I want $50 million!'

d One expert found Pollock's fingerprint on the back of the painting.

e A film company made a film about Teri and the painting.

f An art teacher said the painting was by the famous artist, Jackson Pollock.

Jackson Pollock 1912–1956

It's a Jackson

Pollock!

$9 million?

3 Read and complete the newspaper article with the irregular verbs from exercise 1.

Helen Byers in Los Angeles reports

WHO IS JACKSON POLLOCK?

Teri Horton, a 60-year-old lady from Los Angeles, (**1**) _went_ shopping in San Bernardino, a town in California, USA. She (**2**) _was_ in a charity shop when she (**3**) _____ a colourful, modern painting. She (**4**) _____ it for $5.

An art teacher saw the painting and (**5**) _____ it was by the American artist, Jackson Pollock. 'Who is Jackson Pollock?' said Teri. She (**6**) _____ no idea that he was a very famous modern painter.

Many art experts (**7**) _____ to her house to see the painting. Some said that it wasn't a 'Pollock', but one expert, Peter Paul Biró, (**8**) _____ Pollock's fingerprint on the back. Biró said, 'This is a real Pollock painting'.

A rich businessman was happy to pay $9 million for it, but Teri said: 'No! I want $50 million.'

In 2007, a Canadian TV company (**9**) _____ a film about Teri and the painting. It is now for sale in an art gallery in Toronto. Price: $50 million!

Teri Horton with Pollock painting

Read the article aloud with a partner.
T 9.12 Listen and check.

4 Look at the pictures only and tell the story again.

VOCABULARY
have, do, go

1 Look at the words that go with *have*, *do*, and *go*.

They **have lunch** at 1.00.

I always **do my homework** in bed.

My parents **go shopping** on Saturday afternoon.

2 Write the words in the box next to the correct verb, *have*, *do*, or *go*.

~~shopping~~	~~lunch~~	~~my homework~~
a shower	the housework	on holiday
for a walk	some exercise	home
a good time	breakfast	to work

have
lunch
_____
_____
_____

do
my homework
_____
_____

go
shopping
_____
_____
_____

3 Write the past of *have*, *do*, and *go*.

went	had	did

Present	Past
have	
do	
go	

4 Complete the sentences with *went*, *had* or *did*.

1 Yesterday I met my mother at one o' clock and we __had__ lunch in a restaurant.

2 I hate doing housework but last Sunday I _____ a lot because my house was a mess.

3 Yesterday was a lovely day so I _____ for a walk in the park.

4 Usually I walk but yesterday I _____ to work by bus.

5 On Saturday night I went to a great party. I _____ a really good time.

6 I _____ a lot of exercise yesterday. I went to the gym.

7 The party wasn't very good so we _____ home early.

T 9.13 Listen and check.

Talking about you

5 Complete the sentences with what *you* did.

1 Yesterday I __had__ a shower at _____ o' clock.

2 This morning I _____ breakfast at _____ o' clock. I had coffee and _____.

3 Last Saturday I _____ shopping and I bought _____.

4 Last weekend I _____ my homework at _____ o' clock on _____.

5 Last year I _____ on holiday to _____.

6 Tell a partner what you did.

EVERYDAY ENGLISH
When's your birthday?

1 These are the months of the year. What is the correct order?

January _____

_____

_____

_____

_____

_____

_____

_____

_____

_____

_____

December _____

September

~~January~~

April   March

November

August

October

February

May

July

June   ~~December~~

T 9.14 Listen and check. Say the months round the class.

2 Which month is your birthday? Tell the class.

> My birthday's in September.

> So is my birthday!

How many birthdays are in each month?
Which month has the most?

3 **T 9.15** Listen and repeat the numbers.

first (**1st**)	second (**2nd**)	third (**3rd**)
fourth (**4th**)	fifth (**5th**)	sixth (**6th**)
seventh (**7th**)	eighth (**8th**)	ninth (**9th**)
tenth (**10th**)	eleventh (**11th**)	twelfth (**12th**)
thirteenth (**13th**)	fourteenth (**14th**)	fifteenth (**15th**)

4 Say these numbers.

16th 17th 18th 19th 20th 21st 22nd 23rd
24th 25th 26th 27th 28th 29th 30th 31st

T 9.16 Listen and check.

5 **T 9.17** Listen and write the numbers. Practise them.

the _____ of January
the _____ of March
the _____ of April
the _____ of May
the _____ of June
the _____ of August
the _____ of November
the _____ of December

> **!** **We say:**
> the tenth of April
>
> **We write:**
> 10 April
> April 10
> 10/4/09
>
> **Americans write:**
> 4/10/09

6 When is your birthday? Do you know the time you were born? Ask and answer in groups.

> When's your birthday?

> It's on the third of March.

> What time were you born?

> At two o'clock in the morning.

Tell the class.

> I was born in 1982 on the twentieth of July at two o'clock in the morning.

7 **T 9.18** Sing *Happy Birthday!* to Sarah.

10 We had a great time!

Past Simple – regular and irregular • Questions and negatives •
Sport and leisure • Going sightseeing

1 What day is it today? What day was it yesterday?

2 Match a sentence with a time expression.

We're at school	yesterday.
I went to the US	now.
I did my homework	in 2002.

3 What is the Past Simple of these irregular verbs?

| get | have | go | buy | do | see |

YESTERDAY WAS SUNDAY
Past Simple – regular and irregular

1 **T 10.1** Listen to Angie. Tick (✓) the things she did yesterday. What day was it?

GRAMMAR SPOT

1 Write the Past Simple of these regular verbs. What are the last two letters?

/t/	cook	**cooked**	watch	_____
/d/	play	_____	listen	_____
/ɪd/	start	_____	want	_____

T 10.2 Listen and repeat. Careful with the pronunciation of *-ed*.

2 The Past Simple is always the same.
I/you/he/she/it/we/they **played**

▶▶ **Grammar Reference 10.1 p127**

Yesterday she . . .

- ✓ got up late
- ☐ had a big breakfast
- ☐ played tennis
- ☐ went shopping
- ☐ bought some clothes
- ☐ stayed at home
- ☐ went for a walk
- ☐ cleaned her flat
- ☐ listened to music
- ☐ did some work
- ☐ saw some friends
- ☐ watched TV
- ☐ cooked a meal
- ☐ went to bed early

2 Tell the class what she did.

> Yesterday she got up late and had ... Then she ...

3 Underline the things in the list that *you* did last Sunday. Tell a partner.

> Last Sunday I got up ... and I went ... I saw ...

Questions and negatives

1 It is Monday morning. Angie and Rick are at work.
T 10.3 Listen and complete their conversation.

A Hi, Rick. __Did__ you __have__ a good weekend?

R Yes, I did, thanks.

A What _____ you do yesterday?

R Well, I got up early and I _____ tennis with some friends.

A You _____ up early on Sunday!

R Well, yes, it was such a lovely day.

A Where _____ you _____ tennis?

R In the park. We _____ lunch in the café there.

A Oh, great! _____ you _____ out in the evening?

R No, I didn't. I _____ a meal for my sister.

A Mmm! What _____ you _____ ?

R Roast beef. It was delicious! What about you, Angie? Did _you_ have a good weekend?

2 **T 10.4** Listen and repeat Angie's questions.

Did you **have** a good weekend?
What **did** you **do** yesterday?
Where **did** you **play** tennis?
Did you **go out** in the evening?
What **did** you **have**?

Work with a partner. Practise the conversation in exercise 1.

3 **T 10.5** Listen to Rick asking Angie about _her_ weekend. Complete his questions.

1 What/do on Saturday? **What did you do on Saturday?**
2 Who/see at the party?
3 … go out/Sunday?
4 … do anything/Sunday evening?

Listen again. What _did_ Angie do?

4 **T 10.6** Listen and repeat. What _didn't_ Angie do?

I didn't go out because I was too tired
I didn't do much on Sunday.
I didn't go to bed late.

5 Say three things Angie and Rick _didn't_ do.
Angie: tennis/walk/music   **Rick:** late/shopping/TV
Angie didn't play tennis.   **Rick didn't get up late.**

> ### GRAMMAR SPOT
>
> 1 Questions in the Past Simple use _did_. Complete the questions.
>
> _____ you **go out**?
> Where _____ she **go**?
> What _____ you **do**?
>
> 2 Negatives use _didn't_. Complete the negatives.
> They _____ **go** to work.
> We _____ **watch** TV.
>
> ▶▶ Grammar Reference 10.2 p127

6 Work with a partner. Say what you did and didn't do last night.

What did you do last night?
I didn't do much.
I stayed at home.

PRACTICE

Grammar

1 Complete the sentences in the Past Simple.

1 I _played_ (**play**) tennis on Sunday.

2 Yesterday we _____ (**have**) lunch in the park.

3 She _____ (**do**) her homework on the bus.

4 I _____ (**not clean**) my flat last weekend.

5 'Where _____ he _____ (**buy**) his new computer?'
  'He _____ (**buy**) it on the Internet.'

6 'What _____ you _____ (**do**) last night?'
  'I _____ (**not go**) out. I _____ (**go**) to bed early.'

Did you have a good weekend?

2 Look at the questionnaire. What activities are in the pictures?

3 Put a tick (✓) next to the things *you* did last weekend.

4 Ask your teacher the questions. Put a tick (✓) next to the things she/he did.

> Did you go to the cinema?
>> Yes, I did./No, I didn't.

5 Ask a partner the questions. Put a tick (✓) next to the things she/he did.

Tell the class about you and your partner.

> Maria went to the cinema, but I didn't. I went shopping.

questionnaire
Last weekend

Did you . . . ?	You	Teacher	Partner
go to the cinema	☐	☐	☐
go shopping	☐	☐	☐
have a meal in a restaurant	☐	☐	☐
see your friends	☐	☐	☐
play football	☐	☐	☐
watch TV	☐	☐	☐
go to a party	☐	☐	☐
do a lot of homework	☐	☐	☐
do a lot of housework	☐	☐	☐

Making conversation

6 We ask questions to show we are interested.

We went to the cinema last night.

Oh, really? What did you see?

Was it good?

Who was in it?

Reply to these lines with a question.

1 'I went shopping yesterday.'
'Really? _What did you buy?_ '

2 'We went to that new Italian restaurant last night.'
'Mmm! (What/have?) _____?'

3 'We saw a lot of our friends in the coffee bar.'
'Oh! (Who/see?) _____?'

4 'I played tennis at the weekend.'
'Oh, really? (Where/play?) _____?'

5 'The party on Saturday was great!'
'Oh, good! (What time/leave?) _____?'

T 10.7 Listen and check.

7 Work with a partner. Read the example conversation.

A I went shopping yesterday.
B Really? Where did you go?
A Oxford Street.
B Oh! What did you buy?
A Well, I wanted a new coat, and I went into Selfridges.
B Did you find one?
A Yes, I did. I found a beautiful black one. It was only £50!

Choose one of the conversations in exercise 6 and make it longer.
T 10.8 Listen and compare.

Time expressions

8 Complete the time expressions using a word from the box.

at	in	on	last

I went there . . .

_on_	Monday
_____	night
_____	8 o'clock
_____	week
_____	2007
_____	year
_____	Sunday morning

Check it

9 Tick (✓) the correct sentence.

1 ☐ She bought an expensive car.
☐ She buyed an expensive car.

2 ☐ I played tennis on Sunday.
☐ I play tennis on Sunday.

3 ☐ Did they went shopping yesterday?
☐ Did they go shopping yesterday?

4 ☐ What did you do last weekend?
☐ What did you last weekend?

5 ☐ 'Did you like the film?' 'Yes, I liked.'
☐ 'Did you like the film?' 'Yes, I did.'

6 ☐ I saw John last night.
☐ I saw John on last night.

Really?

Oh, wow!

What...?

Where...?

Who...?

Oh good!

How...?

VOCABULARY AND SPEAKING
Sport and leisure

1 What are the activities in the photos?

- [2] tennis
- [ ] football
- [ ] skiing
- [ ] golf
- [ ] sailing
- [ ] windsurfing
- [ ] rugby
- [ ] ice-skating
- [ ] cards
- [ ] walking
- [ ] swimming
- [ ] dancing
- [ ] cycling
- [ ] fishing
- [ ] horse-riding

2 Write the activities in the correct column.

I play tennis.   *I go skiing.*

play	go + -ing
tennis	skiing

3 Work with a partner. Ask and answer questions about the activities.

Do you play tennis?

Yes, I do.

When did you last play?

Last week.

Do you go skiing?

No, I don't.

4 Tell the class about your partner.

Alicia doesn't play tennis, but she goes skiing. She went skiing in Switzerland last year.

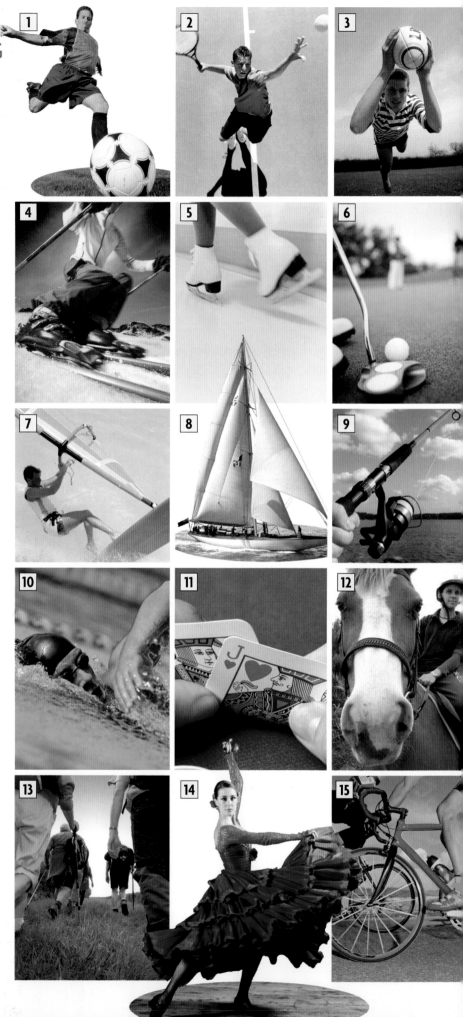

LISTENING AND SPEAKING
Jack and Millie's holiday

1 Say the months of the year.

| January | February | ... |

In your country, what months are ...?

| spring | summer | autumn | winter |

2 When do you usually go on holiday?

> I usually go on holiday in summer.

3 **T 10.9** Listen to Jack and Millie talking about their holidays. <u>Underline</u> what they say.

They usually . . .	But last year they . . .
go in *summer* / *spring*.	went in *autumn* / *winter*.
go to *Italy* / *India*.	went to *Canada* / *Colorado*.
stay in *a hotel* / *a villa*.	stayed in *a hotel* / *a house*.
eat *at home* / *with friends*.	went out to *restaurants* / *diners*.
go *swimming* / *sailing*.	went *skiing* / *ice-skating*.
play *golf* / *cards*.	*stayed in* / *went out* every night.
have / *don't have* a good time.	*had* / *didn't have* a good time.

4 Ask and answer questions with a partner about Jack and Millie's holidays.

- When / go?
- Where / go?
- Where / stay?
- Where / eat?
- What / do?
- ... have a good time?

> When do they usually go on holiday?
> In summer.
> When did they go last year?
> In winter.
> Where ... ?

5 Complete the sentences about their last holiday.

1 Last year Jack and Millie __didn't go__ on holiday in summer. They __went__ in winter.

2 They _____ to Italy. They _____ to Colorado.

3 They _____ in a hotel. They _____ in a villa.

4 They _____ at home. They _____ in restaurants.

5 They _____ skiing. They _____ swimming.

T 10.10 Listen and check.

SPEAKING AND WRITING
My last holiday

1 What is your favourite kind of holiday?
What do you like doing? ✓
What don't you like doing? ✗

- [ ] sitting on the beach
- [ ] camping by a lake.
- [ ] relaxing in the sun
- [ ] going skiing
- [ ] walking in the mountains
- [ ] sightseeing in famous cities
- [ ] visiting museums
- [ ] playing sports

Compare your choices with a partner.

2 What did you do on your last holiday?
Ask and answer questions with your partner.

- Where . . . go?
- When . . . go?
- Where . . . stay?
- What . . . do every day?
- . . . have good weather?
- What . . . do in the evening?
- What . . . eat?
- . . . meet nice people?

> **Where did you go?**
>
> **I went to France.**
>
> **When did you go?**
>
> **Last year. / Two years ago.**

3 Tell the class about your partner.

> **Carl went sightseeing in Rome last June / six months ago.**

sightseeing

beach

walking

camping

GRAMMAR SPOT

ago

two years ago means *two years before now.*

I met James **ten years ago.**

I went to New York **six weeks ago.**

Sally phoned **five minutes ago.**

Writing

4 Write about your last holiday. Read it to the class.

My last holiday

Last ..., I went on holiday to ... I went with ... We stayed in ...

Every day we ... Sometimes we ... Once we ... We met ...

The food was ... and the weather was ...

We had a ... time.

EVERYDAY ENGLISH
Going sightseeing

1 Write the names of two cities and the dates when you were a tourist there.

London, July 2005.   **Paris, April 2009.**

Show a partner. Talk about the cities.
What did you do there? What did you see? What did you buy?

> I went to …

> We visited …

> We saw …

> I bought …

2 〔T 10.11〕 Listen and complete the conversations in a Tourist Office.

1   **A**   Hello. Can I _____ _____ ?

    B   Yes. _____ _____ have a map of the city, please?

    A   Of course. Here you are.

    B   Can you _____ _____ where we are on the _____ ?

    A   Yes. We're _____ in Regent Street in the city _____ .

2   **C**   We want to go on a _____ tour of the _____ .

    A   That's fine. The next bus _____ at 10 o'clock. It _____ about an hour and a half.

    C   Where does the bus go from?

    A   It _____ _____ Trafalgar Square, but you can get _____ and _____ when you want.

3   **D**   I want to visit the British Museum. What time does it _____ ?

    A   It opens at 10 in the morning and _____ at 5.30 in the evening.

    D   _____ _____ is it to get in?

    A   It's _____ .

Work with a partner. Practise the conversations.

3 When people go sightseeing in your town, where do they go? What is there to do in your town?

> We have a beautiful cathedral.

> There's a park and a zoo.

> Visitors go to the market/ the old town /the square …

Roleplay

4 Roleplay a conversation in a Tourist Office with your partner.

Student A

You are a tourist at the Tourist Office.

Ask for information.

Student B

You work in the Tourist Office in your home town.

Give information.

> Hello. I want to go on a tour of the town … see the exhibition … visit the castle …

> That's fine. You can …

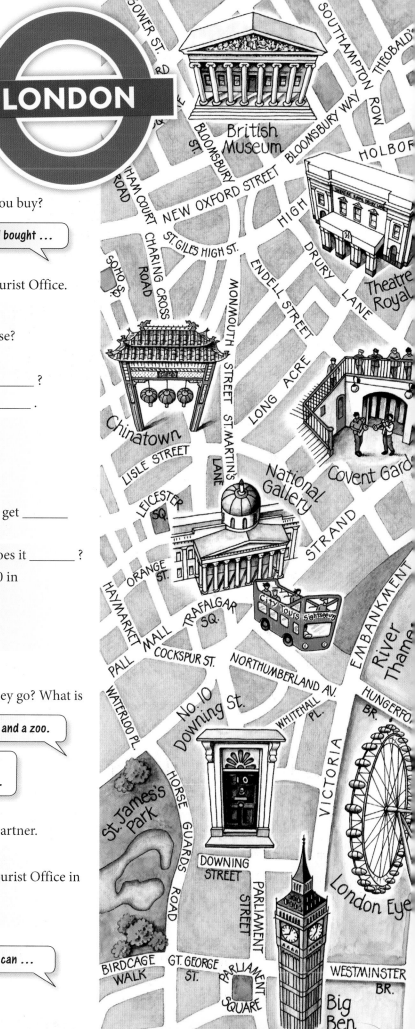

11

I can do that!

can/can't • Adverbs • Adjective + noun • Everyday problems

STARTER

Do you have a computer? Do you use it for ...?
• work • the Internet • computer games • shopping • emails
Talk to a partner. Tell the class.

4 George

5 Lola

WHAT CAN THEY DO?
can/can't

1 Match the words and photos.

> pilot farmer schoolboy athlete
> ~~interpreter~~ grandmother architect

1 Marcus
interpreter

6 Oliver

7 Margaret

2 Laura

2 Complete the sentences with *a* or *an* and a word from exercise 1.

1 Marcus is __an interpreter__ . He can speak French and German fluently.
2 Laura is _____ . She can draw well.
3 Justin is _____ . He can fly 747 jumbo jets.
4 George is _____ . He can drive a tractor.
5 Lola is _____ . She can run very fast.
6 Oliver is _____ . He can use a computer really well.
7 Margaret is Oliver's _____ . She can make fantastic cakes.

T 11.1 Listen and check. Practise the sentences.

3 Justin

3 Tell a partner what you can do from exercise 2.

> I can use a computer
> and I can draw.

Questions and negatives

1 [T 11.2] Listen and repeat the questions and answers.

Can Marcus **speak** French?   Yes, he can.
Can you **speak** French?   Yes, I can.

Can Laura **draw** well?   Yes, she can.
Can you **draw** well?   No, I can't. I can't draw at all!

(?)

2 Ask and answer more questions with a partner. First ask about the people, then ask about your partner.

Can Lola run fast? — Yes, she can.

Can you run fast? — No, I can't.

GRAMMAR AND PRONUNCIATION

1 *Can/Can't* have the same form for all persons.

| I / You / He / She / It / We /They | **can** **can't** | draw. |

2 [T 11.3] Listen and repeat the different pronunciations of *can* and *can't*.

/kən/   /kɑːnt/
He **can** speak Spanish.   They **can't** draw.

/kən/   /kæn/
Can you drive?   Yes, I **can**.

▶▶ **Grammar Reference 11.1–11.2 p128**

Of course I can!

3 [T 11.4] Read and listen to Oliver and Dominique. Complete the conversation.

Dominique Can you use a computer, Oliver?

Oliver Yes, of course I _____! All my friends can. I _____ a computer at home in my bedroom and we use computers at _____ all the time.

D That's great. What other things can you _____?

O Well, I can _____ fast, very fast, and I can draw a bit. I can _____ really good cars but I _____ drive them of course! I can draw good planes, too. When I'm big I want to be a pilot and _____ 747s.

D Excellent. Now, I know you can speak French.

O Yes, I _____. I can speak French fluently because my dad's French. We sometimes _____ French at home.

D Can you speak any other languages?

O No, I _____. I can't speak German or Spanish, just French – and English of course! And I can cook! I can _____ cakes. My grandma makes fantastic cakes and I sometimes help her. Yesterday we made a big chocolate cake!

[T 11.4] Listen again and check. Practise the conversation with a partner.

4 Answer the questions about Oliver.

1 What can Oliver do? What can't he do?
2 Does he use a computer at school?
3 What does he want to be when he's big?
4 Why can he speak French well?
5 What did he do yesterday?

PRACTICE

Pronunciation

1 **T 11.5** Listen and underline *can* or *can't*.

1 I *can* / *can't* ski quite well.
2 She *can* / *can't* speak German at all.
3 He *can* / *can't* speak English fluently.
4 Why *can* / *can't* you come to my party?
5 We *can* / *can't* understand our teacher.
6 They *can* / *can't* read music.
7 *Can* / *Can't* I have an ice-cream, please?
8 *Can* / *Can't* cats swim?

T 11.5 Listen again and repeat.

She can speak Spanish very well!

2 **T 11.6** Jenni Spitzer is American, but she lives in Argentina. Listen and tick (✓) the things she can do.

Can ... ?	Jenni	You	T	S
speak Spanish	☐	☐	☐	☐
speak German	☐	☐	☐	☐
dance	☐	☐	☐	☐
play the guitar	☐	☐	☐	☐
play a musical instrument	☐	☐	☐	☐
ride a horse	☐	☐	☐	☐
play golf	☐	☐	☐	☐
cook	☐	☐	☐	☐

3 Complete Jenni's sentences with words from the box.

very well	a little bit	really well
(not) at all	quite well	fluently

1 I can speak Spanish _____ .

2 I can speak German _____ .

3 My friends can play the guitar _____ .

4 I can dance _____ .

5 I can ride _____ .

6 I can't cook _____ .

T 11.6 Listen again and practise the sentences.

GRAMMAR SPOT

1 Adverbs can come after the verb.
   She can run **fast**.   He plays the guitar **well**.

2 Regular adverbs end in *-ly*.
   She can speak Spanish **fluently**.   Please speak **slowly**.

▶▶ Grammar Reference 11.3 p128

Jenni Spitzer

Talking about you

4 Complete the chart in exercise 2 about *you*. Then ask and answer the questions with the teacher and another student.

> Can you speak Spanish?

> A little bit. Can you?

> I can't speak Spanish at all.

5 Compare yourself with the teacher and other students.

> Isabel and I can dance very well.
> She can cook, too, but I can't cook at all.

REQUESTS AND OFFERS
Can I help you?

1 Look at the pictures. Use the words to write questions with *Can … ?*

2 Match these answers with the questions in exercise 1.

a **3** Sorry. I can't. It's my grandma's birthday on Saturday.

b ___ It's about three thirty.

c ___ Yes, of course. Here you are.

d ___ Yes, please. I want to buy this postcard.

e ___ Oh, yes please! That's so kind of you!

f ___ I'm sorry. Is this better? Can you understand me now?

T 11.7 Listen and check.

3 Practise the questions and answers with a partner. Continue the conversations.

Can you tell me the time, please?

It's about three thirty.

Thank you.

That's OK.

Check it

4 Tick (✓) the correct sentence.

1 ☐ I no can understand.
 ☐ I can't understand.

2 ☐ He can drive a tractor.
 ☐ He cans drive a tractor.

3 ☐ Can you swim fast?
 ☐ Do you can swim fast?

4 ☐ We can to play tennis quite well.
 ☐ We can play tennis quite well.

5 ☐ You speak Italian very good.
 ☐ You speak Italian very well.

6 ☐ He plays very well the piano.
 ☐ He plays the piano very well.

1 Can I help you **?**

2 **?**

3 **?**

4 **?**

5 **?**

6 **?**

READING AND LISTENING
The Internet

1 What are these websites for?
What does 'www' mean?

www.bbc.co.uk

www.londontheatre.com

www.google.com

www.blogger.com

www.youtube.com

www.football365.com

2 Match the verbs and nouns.

Verbs	Nouns
listen to	a newspaper
watch	a bill
play	an email
pay	friends
read	chess
chat to	a hotel
send	TV
book	the radio

Which of these things can you do on
the Internet?

3 What do you know about the Internet?
Discuss these questions.

- When did the Internet start?
- Why did it start?
- What can people do on the Internet?

4 **T 11.8** Read and listen to the text about the
Internet. Answer the questions in exercise 3.

5 Are the sentences true (✓) or false (✗)?
Correct the false (✗) sentences.

1 The Internet started in the 1970s.
2 Telephone companies started it.
3 It started in America.
4 In the 1980s, scientists sent messages
between computers.
5 There is an international computer
language.

You can do more and more on the Internet!

➤ Its history

The Internet started in the 1960s. The United States
Department of Defense started it because they
wanted a computer network to help the American
military. In the 1970s, scientists worked on it and
learnt how to send messages between computers.
Then in the 1980s, telephone companies made it
possible to communicate on the computer network
in many more countries. An international computer
language was born, and the Net went worldwide.

➤ Millions of uses

You can use the Internet for millions of things.
You can 'google' for information about anything
and everything; **you can** buy and sell clothes and
cars; **you can** book a hotel, a holiday, or tickets for
the cinema; **you can** pay your bills; **you can** watch
your favourite TV programme; **you can** play chess
with a partner in Moscow; **you can** 'chat' to your
friends and share photographs on *Facebook*;
you can write a blog about your life.

You can...
the list is endless!

What do you do on the Internet?

6 **T 11.9** Listen to the people. When and why do they use the Internet? Complete the information.

Charlotte, 14

When? *every day*

Why? *help with homework*

Lauren, 20

When? _____

Why? _____

Santiago, 23

When? _____

Why? _____

Alan Krum, 47

When? _____

Why? _____

Oliver, 10

When? _____

Why? _____

Edna, 71

When? _____

Why? _____

T 11.9 Listen again and check.

7 'The list is endless!'

Work in groups. What different things do you use the Internet for? What are your favourite websites? Tell the class.

VOCABULARY AND SPEAKING
Adjective + noun

1 Work with a partner. Match the groups of adjectives with the nouns.

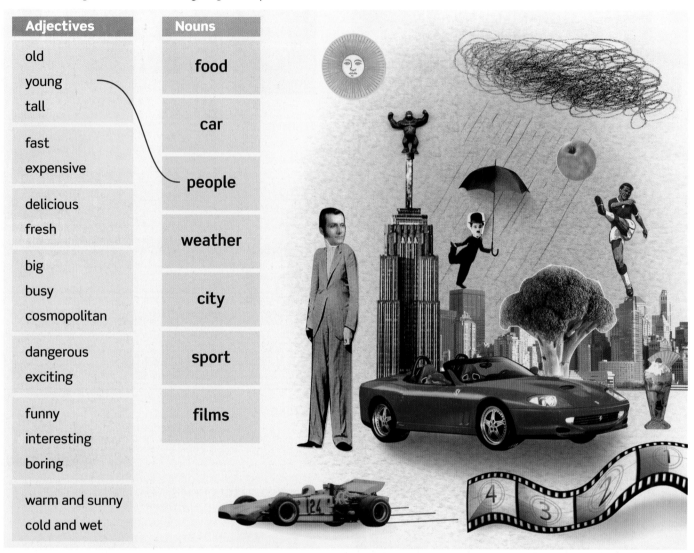

Adjectives	Nouns
old young tall	food
fast expensive	car
delicious fresh	people
big busy cosmopolitan	weather
dangerous exciting	city
funny interesting boring	sport
warm and sunny cold and wet	films

2 Complete the sentences with words from exercise 1. Compare answers with a partner.

1 A Ferrari is _____ .

2 'How _____ is your brother?'
   'He's very _____, 1.9 metres.'

3 I think motor racing is a _____ .

4 Can I have a _____ orange juice, please?

5 New York is a very _____ .

6 Charlie Chaplin made some very _____ .

7 We can't go for a walk, it's too _____ .

T 11.10 Listen and compare. Look at the tapescript on p120 and practise the conversations.

3 Work in groups. Think of examples of these things.

- an **expensive car** and a **cheap car**

- a **dangerous sport** and a **safe sport**

- an **old city** and a **modern city**

- an **old film star** and a **young film star**

- a **funny film** and a **boring film**

Compare your lists.

EVERYDAY ENGLISH
Everyday problems

1 Look at the pictures. Who has a problem with … ?

- [2] computers
- [ ] directions
- [ ] a ticket machine
- [ ] arriving late
- [ ] a lost passport
- [ ] an accident

2 Match the lines with the pictures.

- [4] *I can't find it anywhere!*
- [ ] *This machine doesn't work!*
- [ ] *I'm lost!*
- [ ] *I'm so sorry I'm late!*
- [ ] *I can't get on the Internet!*
- [ ] *Are you all right?*

3 **T 11.11** Listen and complete the conversations.

1 **A** Excuse me! Can you help me? I'm _____!
  B Where do you _____ to go?
  A Grand Central Station.
  B Turn left onto Park Avenue. It's _____ on.
  You _____ miss it.

2 **A** Oh no!
  B What's the _____?
  A There's something _____ with my computer. I can't _____ the Internet, so I can't send my emails.
  B Turn everything off and try _____.
  That sometimes _____.

3 **A** Excuse me! This ticket machine _____.
  B Did you _____ the green button?
  A Oh! No, I didn't.
  B Ah, well. Here's your _____.
  A Thank you very much.

4 **A** Come on! It's time to go to the airport.
  B But I _____ my passport! I can't find it anywhere!
  A You _____ it in your bag.
  B Did I? Oh, yes. _____ it is! Phew!

5 **A** Are you _____?
  B Yes, I think so.
  A Does your arm hurt?
  B It hurts _____, but I think it's OK.

6 **A** I'm so sorry _____.
  B It's OK. The film _____ in 15 minutes.
  A I missed the _____.
  B I told you, it doesn't _____. Come on!
  Let's go.

T 11.11 Listen and check. Practise the conversations.

4 Learn two conversations and act them to the class.

12 Please and thank you

I'd like – *some/any* • In a restaurant • Signs all around

1 Match the activities and the places. What can you do where?

Activities	Places
1 _g_ buy a magazine	a post office
2 ___ buy bread, milk, fruit, and meat	b bookshop
3 ___ get US dollars	c bank
4 ___ buy stamps and send a parcel	d chemist's
5 ___ buy a dictionary	e supermarket
6 ___ get a medium latte	f coffee shop
7 ___ buy shampoo and conditioner	g newsagent's

2 Make sentences with *You can . . .*

You can buy a magazine in a newsagent's.

T 12.1 Listen and check.

SAYING WHAT YOU WANT
I'd like . . . , some and *any*

1 **T 12.2** Listen to Adam and complete the conversations. Where is he?

1 A Good _____ . I'd like some ham, please.
  B How much would you like?
  A _____ slices.
  B Would you like anything else?
  A Yes, I'd like some cheese. _____ you _____ any Emmental?
  B I'm afraid we _____ have any Emmental. What about Gruyère?
  A No, thank you. Just the ham then. _____ much is that?

2 C Can I help you?
  A Yes, please, I'_____ like some shampoo.
  C We have lots. Would you _____ it for dry or normal hair?
  A Dry, I think.
  C OK. Try this one. _____ else?
  A Er – oh yeah. I don't have _____ conditioner.
    I'd like _____ conditioner for dry hair, please.
  C Yes, of course. That's £6.90 please.

T 12.2 Listen again and check. Practise the conversations.

2 **T 12.3** Listen to two more conversations with Adam.

	Conversation 1	Conversation 2
Where is he?		
What does he want?		
What are his words?	I'd like ...	

3 Adam has a visitor. Complete their conversations.

1 A What __would__ you _____ to drink?

V A juice. I'_____ _____ an apple juice, please.

A Er … I have _____ orange juice, but I don't have _____ apple juice.

V Don't worry. Orange juice is fine. Thanks.

2 A _____ you _____ something to eat?

V Yeah, OK. A sandwich. A cheese sandwich?

A Er … I don't have _____ cheese. Sorry. I have _____ ham. _____ you _____ a ham sandwich?

V I don't like ham.

A _____ you _____ some cake, then?

V Yes, please. I'd love _____ .

T 12.4 Listen and check. Practise the conversations.

Roleplay

4 You have a friend at your house. Make him or her feel at home! Offer some of these things.

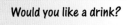

- a drink
- a coffee
- something to eat
- a glass of wine
- some ice-cream

> Would you like a drink?
>
> Yes, please.
>
> What would you like?
>
> A beer, please.

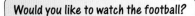

- watch the football
- listen to some music
- watch TV
- see the garden
- play some computer games

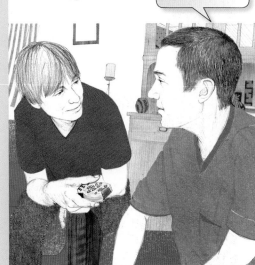

> Would you like to watch the football?
>
> Yes, I'd love to!

PRACTICE

It's my birthday!

1 **T 12.5** Listen to the conversation.
What does the woman want to do? Why is the man *not* happy?

2 Read and complete the conversation with words from the box.

would you like	I'd like	I'd like to (x3)	some

A Hey, isn't it your birthday soon?

B Yeah, next week on the 15th.

A So, what _____ for your birthday?

B I don't know. I don't need anything.

A But, _____ buy you something.

B That's kind but I think _____ forget my birthday this year.

A What? You don't want any presents! Why not?

B Well, I'm 30 next week, and that feels old.

A 30 isn't old. Come on! _____ take you out for a meal
with _____ friends. You can choose the restaurant.

B OK, then. Thank you. _____ that. Just don't tell anyone
it's my birthday.

A Oh, that's silly!

T 12.5 Listen again and check. Practise the conversation.

Birthday wishes

3 **T 12.6** Listen to three people. It's their birthday soon. Complete the chart.

What would they . . .	like for a present?	like to do in the evening?
Kelly		
Mike		
Jade		

4 It's *your* birthday soon! Ask and answer questions about what *you'd* like.

> What would you like for your birthday?

> I'd like an iPod, and some new clothes, ...

> What would you like to do on your birthday?

> I'd like to go out for a meal with some friends.

like and would like

1 What's the difference between these sentences?

I like Coke. *I'd like a Coke.*

2 **T 12.7** Read and listen to the two conversations. Which conversation is about what you like day after day? Which is about what you want to do today?

1 **A** What do you like doing in your free time?
 B I like going to the cinema, and I like playing computer games.
 A Do you like playing . . .?

2 **C** What would you like to do tonight?
 D I'd like to go out. What about you?
 C Great! Would you like to go to the cinema?
 D I'd love to! What's on?

Practise the conversations with a partner.

GRAMMAR SPOT

1 *Like* refers to **always**.
 I **like** tea.
 I **like** go**ing** to the cinema.
2 *'d like* refers to **now** or **soon**.
 I**'d like** a cup of tea, please.
 I**'d like to** go to the cinema tonight.

▶▶ **Grammar reference 12.3 p128**

Talking about you

3 Work with a partner. Make conversations.

> **What do you like doing in your free time?**
>> **I like . . . and I like . . . What about you?**

> **What would you like to do this weekend?**
>> **Well, I'd like to . . . What about you?**

Listening and pronunciation

4 **T 12.8** Listen to the conversations. Tick (✓) the sentences you hear.

1 ✓ Would you like a Coke?
 ☐ Do you like Coke?

2 ☐ I like watching films.
 ☐ I'd like to watch a film.

3 ☐ We like flats with big bedrooms.
 ☐ We'd like a flat with two bedrooms.

4 ☐ What would you like to do?
 ☐ What do you like doing?

5 ☐ I like new clothes.
 ☐ I'd like some new clothes.

Look at **T 12.8** on p121 and practise the conversations.

Check it

5 Tick (✓) the correct sentence.

1 ☐ I like leave early today.
 ☐ I'd like to leave early today.

2 ☐ Do you like your job?
 ☐ Would you like your job?

3 ☐ Would you like tea or coffee?
 ☐ You like tea or coffee?

4 ☐ I'd like any tea, please.
 ☐ I'd like some tea, please.

5 ☐ They like something to eat.
 ☐ They'd like something to eat.

6 ☐ I don't have any money.
 ☐ I don't have some money.

play computer games

eat in a restaurant

watch football

see a film

go fishing

go shopping

sleep a lot

READING AND SPEAKING
You are what you eat

1 Match the food and the pictures.

chicken	fish	salad	pasta	seafood
eggs	rice	bread and jam		breakfast cereal

1		2		3	

4		5		6	

7		8		9	

2 Work in three groups.

Group A   Read about **MASUMI TAKAHASHI**.

Group B   Read about **CAROLINE WEISSMAN**.

Group C   Read about **ADELLA RAMIREZ**.

Answer the questions.

1 Which food in exercise 1 does he/she eat?
2 What does he/she have for breakfast, lunch, and dinner?
3 What time does he/she eat?
4 What does he/she like doing? When? Where?
5 What would he/she like to do?
6 Does he/she do any exercise?

3 Find a student from the other two groups. Compare and swap information.

What do you think?

- Do all three people have a good diet? Do they eat a lot?
- What do *you* eat in a day? When?
- Would you like the food they eat in Japan/New York/Spain?
- What suggestions can you make for a good diet?

   Eat lots of fruit.   **Don't have too much sugar.**

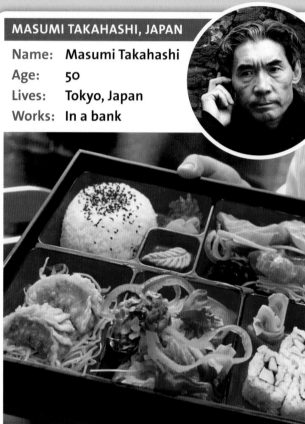

MASUMI TAKAHASHI, JAPAN

Name:	**Masumi Takahashi**
Age:	**50**
Lives:	**Tokyo, Japan**
Works:	**In a bank**

In Japan we eat rice at every meal. For breakfast, we have rice, fish, and soup.

At 12.00 I have *bento*, which is a lunch box. My wife makes this for me every day. There are small dishes of rice, fish, vegetables, eggs, and sometimes meat.

In the evening, we have more fish, maybe with beans. I'd like to eat with my children, but I don't get home till 9.00.

At the weekend, we like doing things together. We go for walks, and have dinner. We eat lots of small dishes. We don't put a lot of food on our plate, so we don't eat too much.

What's on your plate?

Three people from different parts of the world describe what they eat each day.

CAROLINE WEISSMAN, US

Name:	Caroline Weissman
Age:	29
Lives:	Brooklyn, New York
Works:	In a restaurant

I eat little and early. I have toast and cereal for breakfast, and salad for lunch at about 11.30. For dinner I usually eat chicken or fish. If I have a snack between meals, it's always fruit.

I ride my bike to work across Brooklyn Bridge, and run 10 kilometres a day. I'd like to run the New York Marathon this year. I'm a waitress, so I'm on my feet all day.

Too many people in this country don't eat right. They say they don't have time to buy food and cook, so they snack all the time.

At home I like cooking for friends. For me the dinner table is the centre of the home.

ADELLA RAMIREZ, BARCELONA

Name:	Adella Ramirez
Age:	21
Lives:	Barcelona, Spain
Works:	Student

For Spanish people, breakfast is the smallest meal – just some bread and jam and a cup of coffee. We have lunch at about 2.00, and it's a big meal. Perhaps some pasta, then salad, then fish or meat, then a dessert. After lunch, some people have a siesta.

In the evening, I like going to bars with my friends. We have tapas. Tapas are lots of little dishes. Then about 10.00 we go to a restaurant, and maybe have some seafood and rice. Dinner is a lot smaller than lunch. We go to bed very late.

I'd like to do some exercise, go to the gym, but I never have time. Maybe one day!

VOCABULARY AND SPEAKING

In a restaurant

1 Read the menu. What do you like on the menu? What don't you like? Tell a partner.

> I like … and … I don't like … or …

2 **T 12.9** Listen to Liam and Maddy ordering a meal in the CAFÉ FRESCO.

Who says these things? Write L (Liam), M (Maddy), or W (Waiter).

W	Are you ready to order?
____	Well, I am. Are you ready Maddy?
____	Yes, I am. What's the soup of the day?
____	French onion soup.
____	Lovely. I'd like the French onion soup to start, please.
____	And to follow?
____	I'd like the salmon salad with some chips on the side.
____	Thank you. And you sir? What would you like?
____	Er – I'd like the tomato and mozzarella salad, followed by the hamburger and chips.
____	Would you like any side orders?
____	No, thank you. Just the hamburger.
____	And to drink?
____	Sparkling water for me please. What about you Liam?
____	The same for me. We'd like a bottle of sparkling water, please.
____	Fine. I'll bring the drinks immediately.

3 Practise the conversation in groups of three.

Roleplay

4 Work in groups of three. Roleplay being customers and waiters in a restaurant.

CAFÉ FRESCO

STARTERS
Soup of the day	£4.25
Tomato and Mozzarella salad	£5.95

MAINS
Hamburger and chips	£7.25
Fish and chips	£10.25
Salmon salad	£10.95
Spaghetti Bolognese	£9.25
Pizza Margherita	£7.95

SANDWICHES
Chicken and salad	£6.50
Cheese and tomato	£5.95
Egg mayonnaise	£5.95

SIDE ORDERS
Chips	£2.50
Mixed salad	£3.75
Mixed green vegetables	£2.00

DESSERTS
Chocolate cake	£3.85
Apple pie and ice-cream	£3.85

DRINKS
Mineral water, still or sparkling	£1.85

Coke	£2.85	Fruit juice	£2.25
Coffee	£2.00	Tea	£1.65

OPEN 11AM TILL 11PM

EVERYDAY ENGLISH
Signs all around

1 Look at the signs. Where can you see them?

2 Which sign means ...?

1 _f_ You can go in here.
2 __ You can go out here.
3 __ You can't sit here.
4 __ You can't smoke here.
5 __ This machine doesn't work.
6 __ Push this door to open it.
7 __ Pull this door to open it.
8 __ Men can go to the toilet here.
9 __ You can go up or down floors here.
10 __ Women can go to the toilet here.
11 __ You can buy something cheap here.
12 __ Stand and wait here.
13 __ Not open.
14 __ / __ You can't go in here.

3 **T 12.10** Listen to the lines of conversation. Which sign do they go with?

1 ____   2 ____   3 ____   4 ____   5 ____   6 ____   7 ____   8 ____

4 Work with a partner. Write a conversation that goes with a sign. Act it to the class. Can they identify the correct sign?

13 Here and now

Colours and clothes • Present Continuous • Opposite verbs • What's the matter?

1 What are the colours? Write the colours from the box.

blue	red	green
black	white	yellow
brown	grey	

1 _red_   2 _____

3 _____   4 _____

5 _____   6 _____

7 _____   8 _____

What is your favourite colour?
Tell the class.

2 What are the clothes? Write words from the box.

a jacket	trousers	shoes and socks	a scarf	a jumper	boots
trainers	a suit	a shirt and tie	a skirt	a dress	a T-shirt and shorts

1 a jumper   **2** _____   **3** _____   **4** _____

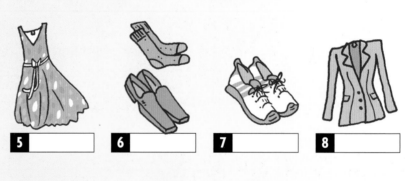

5 _____   **6** _____   **7** _____   **8** _____

9 _____   **10** _____   **11** _____   **12** _____

T 13.1 Listen and repeat.

3 What clothes can you see in the classroom? What colour are they?

Lillian's skirt is black.   *Roberto's shirt is blue.*

WHAT ARE THEY WEARING?
Present Continuous

1 Look at the pictures. Complete the descriptions with the colours and clothes.

> 1 **Nigel**'s wearing a grey _____ and a white _____ . He's reading his emails.
> 2 **Lily**'s wearing a _____ T-shirt and _____ trainers. She's running.
> 3 **Rick**'s wearing _____ jeans and a red _____ . He's playing the guitar.
> 4 **Eva**'s wearing a _____ jacket and _____ boots. She's carrying a black bag.
> 5 **Polly** and **Penny** are wearing yellow _____ and blue _____ . They're eating ice-cream.

T 13.2 Listen and check. Practise the sentences.

GRAMMAR SPOT

1 The **Present Continuous** describes what is happening *now*.

He**'s reading** his emails.
They**'re eating** ice cream.
I**'m sitting** in the classroom.

2 We make the **Present Continuous** with the verb *to be*: *am/is/are* + verb + *-ing*.
Complete the sentences.

I*'m studying* _____ (study) English.
You/We/They _____ (wear) jeans.
She/He _____ (play) in the garden.

▶▶ **Grammar Reference 13.1 p129**

---

2 Work with a partner. Describe someone in the room. Who is it?

> He's wearing a white shirt, blue jeans. He's sitting next to me.

> It's Sergio!

3 Stand up and describe your clothes.

> I'm wearing blue jeans and a black T-shirt.

4 **T 13.3** Listen and repeat the questions.

What**'s** he **wearing?**   What**'s** she **doing?**   What **are** they **doing?** (?)

Ask and answer the questions about the pictures with a partner.

> What's Nigel wearing?

> A grey suit and . . .

> What's he doing?

> He's . . .

PRACTICE

Asking questions

1 Work with a partner. What are the people doing? Ask and answer questions.

What's he doing?

He's cooking.

T 13.4 Listen and check. What extra information do you hear?

2 Mime actions to your partner. Can your partner guess what you are doing?

You're cooking!

Yes, I am. I'm making a cake.

You're playing tennis!

No, I'm not. I'm playing golf.

HE'S ON HOLIDAY AT THE MOMENT
Present Simple and Present Continuous

1 Read about Nigel. Complete the text with the verbs in the box.

go	has	~~works~~	reads
wears	arrives	feels	

Nigel at work

Nigel is a businessman. He **(1)** __works__ from 9.00 to 5.30 every day. He always **(2)** _____ a suit and tie for work. He usually **(3)** _____ lunch at his desk at 1.00. He **(4)** _____ home at about 7.00 every evening and he **(5)** _____ to his children before they **(6)** _____ to bed. He often **(7)** _____ very tired at the end of the day.

T 13.5 Listen and check.

2 Nigel and his family are on holiday in Spain. Nigel is talking with his boss, Bill, on his mobile phone.

T 13.6 Listen to and read the conversation.

Nigel on holiday

Nigel Hello.

Bill Nigel, it's Bill, sorry to call you about work.

N Oh, hi Bill! That's OK.

B First things first, **are** you **having** a good time?

N Yes, we are. We**'re having** a great time.

B **Are** you **staying** in a hotel?

N No, we're not. We**'re staying** in a house with a swimming pool near the beach.

B Wonderful. And your family? **Are** they **enjoying** it?

N Oh, yes. The kids **are swimming** in the pool right now. Can you hear them?

B I can. And **are** you and your wife **relaxing**?

N We are. We**'re sitting** by the pool. Karen**'s sunbathing**, and I**'m reading** a lot. And I**'m not wearing** a suit and tie, just shorts and a T-shirt.

B You're lucky. It**'s raining** again here. Now, I**'m calling** about work …

N OK Bill, what's the problem?

B Well …

GRAMMAR SPOT

Read the sentences.

He **wears** a suit for work.

He**'s wearing** a T shirt.

Which sentence is about *now*?

Which is true day after day but *not* now?

▶▶ **Grammar Reference 13.2 p129**

3 How many true sentences can you make about Nigel's holiday? Compare with your partner.

Nigel		enjoying the holiday.
Karen	is	talking to Bill.
Bill	isn't	calling Nigel.
The children	are	staying in a hotel.
It	aren't	wearing a suit.
They		raining in Spain.
		swimming in the pool.
		relaxing.

4 Work with a partner. Ask and answer the questions about Nigel's holiday.

1 Are they … a good time?
2 Where … staying?
3 What … the children doing?
4 What … Karen doing?
5 What … Nigel doing?
6 Is he … a suit?
7 Why … Bill calling?

> Are they having a good time?

> Yes, they are.

T 13.7 Listen and check.

5 Complete the sentences with the verbs in the Present Simple or Present Continuous.

1 Nigel _lives_____ (live) in a house in London, but now he _'s staying_____ (stay) in a house by the sea.

2 He usually _____ (wear) a suit but today he _____ (wear) shorts.

3 He never _____ (relax) at work but now he _____ (relax) by the pool.

4 Karen _____ (work) in a shop, but today she _____ (enjoy) her holiday.

5 The children _____ (work) hard at school but today they _____ (swim) in the pool.

6 It often _____ (rain) in England and it _____ (rain) there now.

PRACTICE

Questions and answers

1 Make the questions.

1 you/wear/a new jumper?
   Are you wearing a new jumper?

2 we/learn/Chinese?

3 we/sit/in a classroom?

4 you/listen/to the teacher?

5 the teacher/wear/blue trousers?

6 all the students/speak/English?

7 you/learn/a lot of English?

8 it/rain today?

Stand up. Ask and answer the questions.

> Are you wearing a new jumper?

> No, I'm not. It's really old.

A photo of you

2 Bring a photograph of you to class. Say …

- where you are.
- what you're doing.
- who you're with.
- what you're wearing.

Check it

3 Tick (✓) the correct sentence.

1 ☐ I'm wear a blue shirt today.
   ☐ I'm wearing a blue shirt today.

2 ☐ Where are you going?
   ☐ Where you going?

3 ☐ Peter no working this week.
   ☐ Peter isn't working this week.

4 ☐ That's Peter over there. He talks to the teacher.
   ☐ That's Peter over there. He's talking to the teacher.

5 ☐ Heidi is German. She comes from Berlin.
   ☐ Heidi is German. She's coming from Berlin.

6 ☐ Why aren't you having a coffee?
   ☐ Why you no having a coffee?

READING AND LISTENING
This week is different

1 How do very rich people spend their time and money? What don't they do? Compare ideas with the class.

> They often have very big, expensive cars.

> They don't travel by public transport.

2 Read the introduction to the TV programme *The Secret Millionaire*. What do the millionaires do in the programme? Why are they called *secret millionaires*?

THE SECRET MILLIONAIRE

The Secret Millionaire is a programme on TV's Channel 4. Every week a different millionaire leaves his or her comfortable, expensive home and lives and works for ten days with people who aren't rich and need help. The people don't know who he or she is. They are 'secret millionaires'.

Colin Cameron

3 Read about **Colin Cameron**. Complete the questions.

1 When _____ he start his business?
2 Where _____ he live?
3 Does he _____ any children?
4 Why _____ he a lucky man?
5 Who does he _____ to help?

Work with a partner. Ask and answer the questions.

4 Read **This week is different**. Are the sentences true (✓) or false (✗)? Correct the false ones.

1 Colin went to Manchester by bus.
2 He's staying in a flat in the centre of the city.
3 He isn't sleeping in a bedroom.
4 The hostel is for homeless boys and girls.
5 He's helping the boys to read and write.
6 They don't think that he is a good teacher.
7 Colin isn't enjoying the work at all.
8 He wants to give Roger and Margaret a lot of money.

Listening

5 **T 13.8** Listen to four conversations with Colin. Complete the chart.

	Who's he talking to?	What's he talking about?
1		
2		
3		
4		

What do you think?

Discuss the questions.

- How is Colin a typical millionaire? How is he not?
- Why would Colin like his sons to meet the boys?
- Do you think the TV programme is a good idea?

Colin Cameron is this week's millionaire. He started his business 25 years ago when he was 19. He's now worth £60 million and lives with his wife and two teenage sons in a beautiful, big country house. He also has a house in Majorca, and apartments in London and New York. He drives a yellow Lamborghini and even has a private plane. He says:

> "I am a very lucky man. Now I want to help people who are not as lucky as I am, especially young people."

This week is different

Colin left his family last weekend and went by train to Manchester. He is now living in Moss Side, a poor area of the city. He is staying with a married couple, Roger and Margaret Watson. They think he is looking for work in Manchester.

Roger and Margaret

Roger and Margaret live in a small flat on the 8th floor of an apartment block. They only have one bedroom so Colin is sleeping on the sofa in the living room. They run a hostel for homeless teenage boys.

This week Colin is working with the boys in the hostel, an old, grey building in a busy road. Some of the boys can't read and write very well and he is helping them learn so that they can find jobs.

Roger, Margaret and the boys like Colin. They think that he is a good teacher. They have no idea he is a millionaire. Colin says:

> "I'm missing my family a lot but Roger and Margaret are wonderful people. I'm enjoying my time with them very much. I'm learning a lot about life. At the end of the week I want to give them £100,000 to build a new hostel. I'd like to bring my sons here to meet them all."

Boys from the hostel

VOCABULARY AND LISTENING
Opposite verbs

1 Look at the two sentences. <u>Underline</u> the verbs. They are verbs with opposite meaning.

> The teacher's asking us questions.   We're answering them.

2 Match the verbs with their opposites.

1 leave __arrive__	5 love _____	9 get up _____
2 work _____	6 open _____	10 remember _____
3 buy _____	7 turn on _____	11 put on _____
4 walk _____	8 start _____	12 win _____

> play   sell   hate   turn off   ~~arrive~~
> finish   forget   take off
> go to bed   lose   run   close

3 Look at the pictures. Complete the sentences with the opposite verb in the correct form.

1 Please, don't **ask** me any more questions. I can't _____ them.

2 I'm **selling** my old car and I'm _____ a new one.

3 We always **get up** at seven in the morning and _____ at eleven at night.

4 It was cold, so Tom **took off** his T-shirt and _____ a warm jumper.

5 I usually **walk** to school but yesterday I was late so I _____ all the way.

6 John's playing tennis with Peter today. He always **loses**. He never _____ .

7 Don't **turn off** the TV, I'm watching it! Please _____ it _____ again!

T 13.9 Listen and check.

4 **T 13.10** Listen. Write down the opposite verbs in each conversation.

1 __hate__ , __love__   2 _____ , _____   3 _____ , _____   4 _____ , _____   5_____ , _____   6_____ , _____

Look at the tapescript on p122. Practise the conversations.

EVERYDAY ENGLISH
What's the matter?

1 What's the matter with the people? Complete the sentences with words in the box.

| tired | hungry | thirsty | ~~cold~~ | hot | bored | worried | angry | a cold | a headache |

1 She's _cold_ .   2 He's _____ .   3 They're _____ .   4 He's _____ .   5 They're _____ .

6 She's _____ .   7 He's _____ .   8 She's _____ .   9 He has _____ .   10 She has _____ .

T 13.11 Listen and repeat.

2 Complete the conversations with words from exercise 1.

1

A What's the matter?
B I'm _____ and _____ .
A Why don't you have a cup of tea?
B That's a good idea.
A Sit down. I'll make it for you.

2

C What's the matter?
D I have a bad _____ .
C Oh dear! Why don't you take some aspirin?
D I don't have any.
C It's OK. I have some.

T 13.12 Listen and check. Practise the conversations with a partner.

Roleplay

3 Have similar conversations. Use the words from exercise 1 and these ideas.

- go to bed early
- put on a jumper
- have a sandwich
- have a cold drink
- talk to a friend
- watch a video
- sit down and relax
- go to the cinema
- have a cold shower

14 It's time to go!

Future plans • Grammar revision
Vocabulary revision • Social expressions (2)

1 Write the form of transport.

1 _____ 2 _____

3 _____ 4 _____

5 _____ 6 _____

7 _____ 8 _____

2 How do you travel? Where to?

I usually come to school by bus but today I came by car.

Sometimes I travel by . . .

SEVEN COUNTRIES IN SEVEN DAYS!
Future plans

1 **Bill** and **Gloria Bigelow** are from the US. Next week they are going on holiday to Europe. Look at the map and answer the questions.

1 Which seven countries are they going to visit?

2 Where does the holiday begin? Where does it end?

3 How are they travelling?

2 Read the holiday information and check your answers.

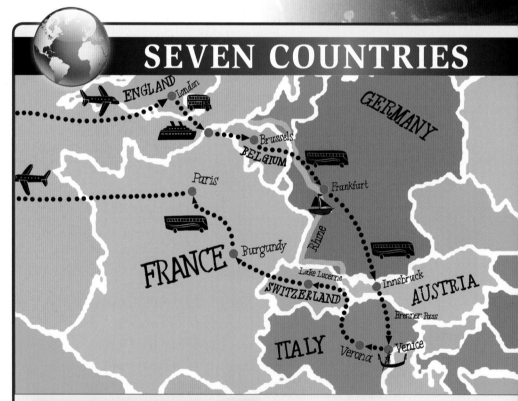

SEVEN COUNTRIES

ENGLAND — London
GERMANY
Brussels
BELGIUM
Frankfurt
Paris
Rhine
FRANCE
Burgundy
Lake Lucerne
Innsbruck
SWITZERLAND
AUSTRIA
Brenner Pass
ITALY
Verona — Venice

HOLIDAY INFORMATION

1 SUNDAY COLUMBUS AIRPORT, OHIO, US – LONDON ENGLAND
Fly overnight to London.

2 MONDAY LONDON, **ENGLAND**
Check into hotel. Bus tour of London, visit Buckingham Palace, the Houses of Parliament, the Tower of London. See the city from the London Eye.

IN SEVEN DAYS

3 TUESDAY LONDON – BELGIUM – FRANKFURT, GERMANY
Early morning start. Ferry across the English Channel and coach through Belgium and into Germany. Evening boat cruise on the River Rhine. Overnight in Frankfurt.

4 WEDNESDAY FRANKFURT – INNSBRUCK, AUSTRIA
By coach down Germany's famous 'Romantic Road' to the Alps and Austria. Overnight in Innsbruck.

5 THURSDAY INNSBRUCK – BRENNER PASS – VENICE, ITALY
South to Italy. Drive over the fantastic 'Europa Bridge' and drive through the Brenner Pass to Venice. Boat ride along the Canals to Piazza San Marco. Overnight in Venice.

6 FRIDAY VENICE – LAKE LUCERNE, SWITZERLAND
Stop in Verona to see Romeo and Juliet's balcony. Drive through the St. Gotthard Tunnel to Switzerland and beautiful Lake Lucerne. Overnight at Lake Lucerne.

7 SATURDAY LAKE LUCERNE – PARIS, FRANCE
The autoroute into France and through Burgundy wine country to Paris. Have dinner in the evening in a Left Bank bistro. Overnight in Paris.

8 SUNDAY PARIS – COLUMBUS AIRPORT, OHIO, US
Morning sightseeing in Paris, the Eiffel Tower, Notre Dame and the Louvre to see the Mona Lisa. Overnight flight back to Columbus, US.

---

3 Read the holiday information again carefully. Complete the sentences.

1 On Sunday they're flying to _____ .
2 On Monday they're going to have a _____ tour of London.
3 On Tuesday they're travelling through _____ and into _____ .
4 On Wednesday they're going to drive down the 'Romantic Road' to the Alps and _____ .
5 On Thursday they're going to _____ over the Europa Bridge.
6 On Friday they're going to _____ in Verona. They're _____ to see Juliet's balcony.
7 On Saturday evening they're _____ dinner in a bistro in Paris.
8 On Sunday morning they're _____ to the Louvre to see the Mona Lisa. In the evening they're _____ back to the US.

T 14.1 Listen and check. Practise the sentences.

Questions

4 **T 14.2** Listen and repeat the questions.

What **are** they **doing** on Sunday?
What **are** they **going to do** on Monday?

5 Complete the questions about Bill and Gloria.

1 What/doing/Tuesday?
2 What/going to do/Wednesday?
3 When/going to drive/the Europa Bridge?
4 What/going to do/Verona?
5 Where/having dinner/Saturday?
6 When/going to the Louvre?
7 When/flying back/the US?

T 14.3 Listen and check. Ask and answer the questions with your partner.

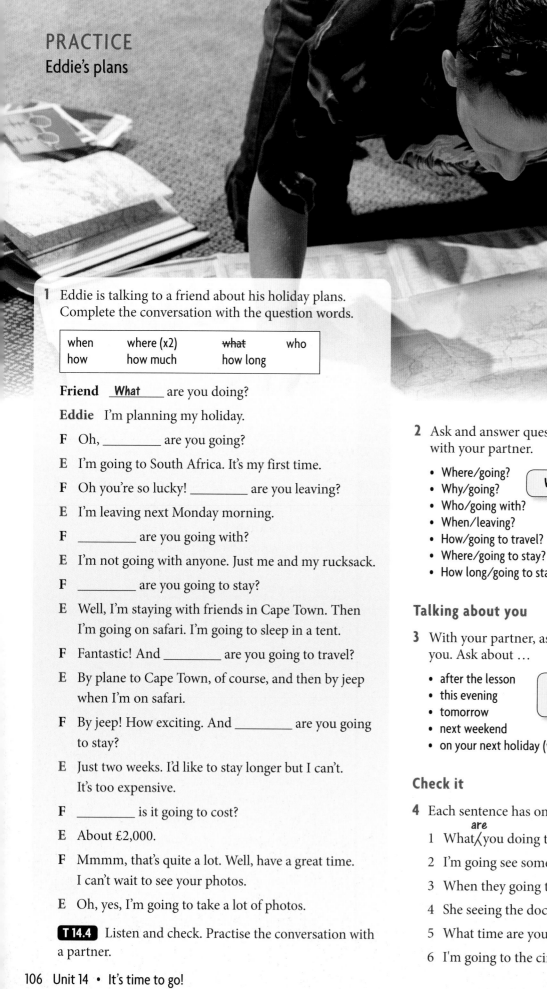

PRACTICE
Eddie's plans

1 Eddie is talking to a friend about his holiday plans. Complete the conversation with the question words.

when	where (x2)	~~what~~	who
how	how much	how long	

Friend __What__ are you doing?

Eddie I'm planning my holiday.

F Oh, _____ are you going?

E I'm going to South Africa. It's my first time.

F Oh you're so lucky! _____ are you leaving?

E I'm leaving next Monday morning.

F _____ are you going with?

E I'm not going with anyone. Just me and my rucksack.

F _____ are you going to stay?

E Well, I'm staying with friends in Cape Town. Then I'm going on safari. I'm going to sleep in a tent.

F Fantastic! And _____ are you going to travel?

E By plane to Cape Town, of course, and then by jeep when I'm on safari.

F By jeep! How exciting. And _____ are you going to stay?

E Just two weeks. I'd like to stay longer but I can't. It's too expensive.

F _____ is it going to cost?

E About £2,000.

F Mmmm, that's quite a lot. Well, have a great time. I can't wait to see your photos.

E Oh, yes, I'm going to take a lot of photos.

T 14.4 Listen and check. Practise the conversation with a partner.

2 Ask and answer questions about Eddie's holiday plans with your partner.

- Where/going?
- Why/going?
- Who/going with?
- When/leaving?
- How/going to travel?
- Where/going to stay?
- How long/going to stay?

> *Where's he going?*
>
> *He's going to South Africa.*
>
> *Why is he going there?*
>
> *Because ...*

Talking about you

3 With your partner, ask and answer questions about you. Ask about ...

- after the lesson
- this evening
- tomorrow
- next weekend
- on your next holiday (where)

> *What are you doing/going to do after the lesson?*

Check it

4 Each sentence has one word missing. Write it in.
1 What⁄you doing this evening? *(are)*
2 I'm going see some friends tonight.
3 When they going to France?
4 She seeing the doctor tomorrow.
5 What time are you to leave?
6 I'm going to the cinema Saturday evening.

VOCABULARY REVISION
Words that go together

1 Match a verb in **A** with words in **B**.

A	B
travel	hard
ride	a photograph
drive	by train
go	dinner with friends
work	a bike
have	sightseeing
take	carefully
do	a suit
pay	your homework
wear	bills on the Internet

Work with a partner. Talk about *your* plans

> I'm going to travel by train next Saturday.

2 Draw a line between words that have a connection.

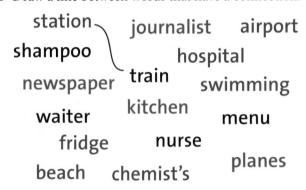

station journalist airport
shampoo hospital
newspaper train swimming
waiter kitchen menu
fridge nurse
beach chemist's planes

Explain the connection.   Trains travel between stations.

3 Three words belong to a group and one is different. Underline the one that is different. Why is it different?

1 train   bus   <u>bridge</u>   motorbike
2 wife   waiter   aunt   grandfather
3 lovely   fantasic   amazing   awful
4 trainers   trousers   socks   boots
5 desk   armchair   sofa   laptop
6 actor   journalist cooker   painter

Pronunciation

4 Write the words in the correct box.

Two syllables

pilot	hotel	women	married
enjoy	shampoo	chocolate	arrive

●●	●●
pilot	hotel

T 14.5 Listen and check.

Three syllables

photograph	designer	assistant	vegetable	magazine
interesting	understand	banana	souvenir	

●●●	●●●	●●●
photograph		

T 14.6 Listen and check.

5 **T 14.7** Listen and <u>underline</u> the two words that rhyme.

1 <u>some</u>   home   <u>come</u>
2 goes   knows   does
3 were   here   her
4 make   steak   speak
5 near   wear   there
6 eat   great   wait

T 14.7 Listen again and check.

1 Put these life events into an order.

____ … went to school

_1_ … was born …

____ … got married

____ … grew up …

____ … studied at university

____ … met a boyfriend/girlfriend

2 Look at the pictures of the people.

T 14.8 Listen to Milena Dušek, Georg Reinhardt, and Archie McCrae talk about their lives. Who talks about …?

- his/her parents
- his/her girlfriend/boyfriend/husband/wife
- his/her studies
- where he/she lives

What do they say?

3 Work in three groups.

Group A	Read about **Milena Dušek**.
Group B	Read about **Georg Reinhardt**.
Group C	Read about **Archie McCrae**.

Read your text quickly. Find one piece of information about his/her past, present, and future. Compare your ideas in your group.

4 Read your text again and answer the questions.

1 Where … born?

2 Where … live? Who … with?

3 Where … grow up?

4 What … parents do? What … wife do?

5 Where … go to school?

6 What … studying at school/university?

7 When … going abroad?

8 What … going to do there?

9 How does … feel about going?

Find a student from the other two groups. Compare and swap information.

Past, Present,

Three people talk about their family,

Milena Dušek

Georg Reinhardt

Archie McCrae

and Future
education, work, and ambitions.

Milena Dušek is Czech. She was born in Prague, where she still lives with her mother and two sisters. She's 18, and she goes to an international school. She is studying English, psychology, and economics.

'My parents are divorced. My father is a journalist, and works for a newspaper called Blesk. My mother works as a chef in a restaurant in the Old Town. I see my father quite often. He lives nearby.'

Milena wants to work in banking. She's going to study business when she's older, so it's important that she speaks very good English. Next summer she's going to London for two months to study at a language school. She's going to stay with an English family, and she's going to learn English for five hours a day.

She's excited about going to London, but a little bit worried, too. 'I hope the family are nice, and I hope I like English food!' she says.

Georg Reinhardt is an architect. He's married, and he lives with his wife, Karlotta, and three children, in Berlin. Karlotta is a housewife, and their three children go to a local gymnasium (school).

'I was born in Frankfurt, where I grew up and went to school. I studied architecture at the University of Munich. I met Karlotta at university, she was a student of modern languages. We moved to Berlin in 1995.'

Georg also teaches architecture. Next year he is moving to America, to teach at the University of California in Berkeley for three years. His family is going with him. They're going to live on the university campus, where there is a school for the children. His wife is going to teach German.

They're all very excited about the trip. 'The kids are learning English. They want to see the Golden Gate Bridge in San Francisco,' says Georg. 'My wife and I are looking forward to living in sunshine all year round.'

Archie McCrae is Scottish. He was born in Glasgow, where he grew up with his parents and his brother and sister. His father is a doctor and his mother works for the reseach company, Bayer.

'I went to Drumchapel High School. I studied biology, chemistry, and physics. At school I met Fiona, and we started going out when we were 16. We studied medicine together at the University of Edinburgh, and now we live in Edinburgh.'

They want to work in developing countries. Next week they're going to Zambia, in Southern Africa, for a year, to work in St Francis' Hospital in the east of the country. They're going to train doctors and nurses in villages near the hospital.

How do they feel about their trip? 'We're very excited, but a bit nervous,' says Archie. 'Zambia is a beautiful country, but very poor. The people are wonderful. I hope we can help them.'

Talking about you

5 When we meet someone for the first time, we sometimes say a little bit about ourselves.

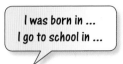

> I was born in …
> I go to school in …

Find the expressions in the box in the texts about Milena, Georg, and Archie. Underline them.

was born	grew up	live with
going to	hope	work as/for
studying/studied		excited about

6 Use the expressions in exercise 5 to write sentences about you.

7 Work with a partner. Imagine you are meeting for the first time.

Tell him/her about yourself.

Ask questions to learn more about him/her.

> Who do you …?
> When did you …?
> What are you going to …?

GRAMMAR REVISION
Tenses

1 Complete the sentences about Archie McCrae from p109 with the verbs in the correct tense.

1 Archie and Fiona __live__ (live) in Edinburgh.
2 Archie _____ (have) a brother and a sister.
3 His mother _____ (work) for a research company, *Bayer*.
4 Archie _____ (grow up) in Glasgow.
5 He _____ (study) medicine at university.
6 He and Fiona _____ (go) to work in Zambia soon.

Questions

2 Complete the questions about Archie.

1 Where __do Archie and Fiona live?__
   They live in Edinburgh.
2 How many _____ ?
   Two, one brother and one sister.
3 Who _____ for?
   A research company called 'Bayer'.
4 Where did _____ ?
   In Glasgow.
5 What _____ ?
   Medicine.
6 Where are _____ ?
   Zambia.

Check it

3 Underline and correct the mistakes.

1 He <u>come</u> from Canada. *comes*
2 I no want to go out.
3 She has 18 years old.
4 Where you live?
5 I went in Italy last year.
6 He have a dog and a cat.
7 I no can understand you.
8 What did you last night?
9 I going see a film tonight.
10 What you do this weekend?

Sentence completion

4 Write the correct answer.

1 I have __some__ homework to do this evening.
   a any   ~~**b**~~ some
2 In our town _____ a big park.
   a there's   **b** it's
3 Who is _____ man talking to Jane?
   a this   **b** that
4 I don't have _____ money. Sorry.
   a any   **b** some
5 Ann, _____ is my brother, Pete.
   Pete, _____ is Ann.
   a this   **b** that
6 My brother Pete is _____ actor.
   a a   **b** an
7 My _____ name is Alice.
   a mothers   **b** mother's
8 You speak _____ .
   a English very well   **b** very well English
9 I have a _____ .
   a car German   **b** German car
10 I'm hungry. _____ a sandwich.
   a I'd like   **b** I like

EVERYDAY ENGLISH
Social expressions (2)

1 **T 14.9** Listen and look at the pictures. Complete the conversations with the words in the boxes.

best	later	luck

1 A Good _____ in the exam! I hope it goes well.

B Thanks. I'll do my _____.

A See you _____. Bye!

matter	so	worry

2 C Oh, no!

D Don't _____. It doesn't _____.

C I'm _____ sorry!

weekend	Same	special

3 E Have a good _____!

F Thanks! _____ to you! What are you doing? Anything _____?

E We're going to a birthday party.

soon	phone

4 G Goodbye! Drive carefully!

H Thanks! I'll _____ you when I arrive.

G See you again _____!

kind	present	to say

5 I I have a _____ for you.

J For me? Why?

I It's just _____ thank you.

J That's so _____ of you!

pleasure	everything	Bye

6 K _____! And thanks for _____!

L It was a _____. We enjoyed having you.

T 14.9 Listen again and check.

2 Work in pairs. Learn the conversations. Stand up! Act the conversations to the class.

Tapescripts

UNIT 1

T 1.1 **T 1.2** see p6

T 1.3 **T 1.4** **T 1.5** see p7

T 1.6 see p8

T 1.7
1 A Hello. My name's Ana. What's your name?
  B My name's Mario.
2 A Max, this is Carla.
  B Hi, Carla.
  C Hello, Max. Nice to meet you.
3 A Hi, Eda. How are you?
  B Fine, thanks, David. And you?
  A Very well, thanks.

T 1.8 **Everyday English**
1 A Good morning!
  B Good morning! What a lovely day!
2 A Good afternoon!
  B Hello. A cup of tea, please.
3 A Goodbye!
  B Bye! See you later!
4 A Good night!
  B Good night! Sleep well!

T 1.9
1 A Good morning! How are you today?
  B Fine, thanks.
2 A Good afternoon!
  B Good afternoon! A cup of coffee, please.
3 A Goodbye! Have a nice day!
  B Thank you. And you. See you later.
4 A Good night! Sleep well.
  B Thank you. And you.

T 1.10 **Vocabulary**
1 a book   7 a hamburger
2 a computer   8 a sandwich
3 a television   9 a camera
4 a phone   10 a photograph
5 a bus   11 a bag
6 a car   12 a house

T 1.11 see p10

T 1.12 see p11

T 1.13 **Plurals**
a five books
b three cars
c eight houses
d seven cameras
e nine photographs
f two sandwiches
g four computers
h six buses
i ten students

T 1.14 see p11

UNIT 2

T 2.1 **T 2.2** **T 2.3** see p12

T 2.4 **Where's he from?**
1 His name's Kevin. He's from the United States.
2 His name's László. He's from Hungary.
3 Her name's Karima. She's from Egypt.
4 Her name's Tatiana. She's from Russia.
5 Her name's Rosely. She's from Brazil.
6 His name's Simon. He's from England.
7 His name's Yong. He's from China.
8 Her name's Hayley. She's from Australia.

T 2.5 see p13

T 2.6 **Cities and countries**
Where's Barcelona?   It's in Spain.
Where's Beijing?   It's in China.
Where's Moscow?   It's in Russia.
Where's Cairo?   It's in Egypt.
Where's Los Angeles? It's in the United States.
Where's São Paulo?   It's in Brazil.
Where's Sydney?   It's in Australia.
Where's Tokyo?   It's in Japan.
Where's Budapest?   It's in Hungary.
Where's London?   It's in England.

T 2.7 **Questions and answers**
R = Rosely, B = Bruno
R Hello, I'm Rosely. What's your name?
B My name's Bruno.
R Hello, Bruno. Where are you from?
B I'm from Brazil. Where are you from?
R Oh, I'm from Brazil, too. I'm from São Paulo.
B Really? I'm from São Paulo, too!
R Oh, nice to meet you, Bruno.

T 2.8
1 C Hello. I'm Claudio. I'm from Italy.
  A Hello, Claudio. I'm Akemi from Japan.
2 C Hello. My name's Charles. What's your name?
  B Hi Charles. I'm Bud. I'm from the United States. Where are you from?
  C I'm from London, in England.
  B Oh, right! I'm from Chicago.
3 L Hi! I'm Loretta. I'm from Sydney, Australia.
  J Hi, Loretta. I'm Jason. I'm from Australia, too.
  L Oh, wow! Are you from Sydney?
  J No, I'm from Melbourne.

T 2.9 **Questions and answers**
1 Where are you from?
  I'm from Brazil.
2 What's her name?
  Her name's Tatiana.
3 What's his name?
  His name's Bruno.
4 Where's he from?
  He's from São Paulo.
5 What's this in English?
  It's a computer.

6 How are you?
  Fine, thanks.
7 Where's Montreal?
  It's in Canada.

T 2.10 see p16

T 2.11 **Where are they from?**
C= Claude, H = Holly
1 C Oh, no! Look at the weather!
  H Ugh! It's awful!
2 H Wow! Look at my hamburger! It's fantastic!
  C My hamburger is really good, too!
3 C What's this building?
  H It's the Empire State Building! It's fantastic!
4 C Wow! Look at Central Park!
  H It's beautiful!

T 2.12 see p17

T 2.13 **Numbers 21 – 30**
twenty-one   twenty-two   twenty-three
twenty-four   twenty-five   twenty-six
twenty-seven   twenty-eight   twenty-nine
thirty

T 2.14
1 12   2 16   3 9   4 17   5 23

T 2.15
1 This is little Becky. She's two.
2 Her name's Naomi. She's seven.
3 He's Nathan. He's fifteen tomorrow.
4 How old is she? She's 26.
5 This is Jeremy. He's 29, nearly 30.

UNIT 3

T 3.1 **Jobs**
1 a teacher   6 a shop assistant
2 a doctor   7 a nurse
3 a bus driver   8 a student
4 a police officer   9 a businessman
5 a builder

T 3.2 **T 3.3** see p18

T 3.4 **Ellie Green**
1 What's her surname?
  Green.
2 What's her first name?
  Ellie.
3 Where's she from?
  England.
4 What's her address?
  29, Victoria Road, Birmingham
5 What's her phone number?
  07700 955031
6 How old is she?
  She's twenty.
7 What's her job?
  She's a student.
8 Is she married?
  No, she isn't.

T 3.5 see p19

T 3.6 *Metro 5 – The audition interview*
I = Interviewer; P = Paul, D = Donny,
All = *Metro 5*
I Hi! Is this your band, *Metro 5*?
P Yes, it is.
I Great! And are you Donny McNab?
P No, I'm not. I'm Paul McNab. This is Donny. He's my brother.
I Ah, yes, sorry. Hi Donny. You're a builder from Scotland right?
D Well, yes, I am a builder but I'm not from Scotland.
I Oh, where are you from?
P&D We're from Ireland.
I Are the other boys from Ireland too?
D No, they aren't. They're all from different countries.
I Oh! Interesting! And are they all builders?
D No, they aren't. Paul's a bus driver and …
P Yeah, I'm a bus driver and Ronan's a nurse and Bo and Edson are students.
I Interesting! And Donny, are you the singer in the band?
D Yes, I am. Well, we're all singers!
I Oh right! Nice to meet you. Good luck to you all!
All Thank you very much.

T 3.7 Questions and answers
1 What's the band's name?
Metro 5.
2 Are Paul and Donny brothers?
Yes, they are.
3 Are they from Scotland?
No, they aren't.
4 Are the other boys from Ireland?
No, they aren't.
5 Are they all builders?
No, they aren't.
6 Are they all singers?
Yes, they are.

T 3.8

Diego Hernandez
I = Interviewer, D = Diego
I Good morning.
D Hello.
I What's your name, please?
D My name's Diego Hernandez.
I Thank you. And where are you from, Diego?
D I'm from Mexico, from Mexico City.
I Thank you. And your telephone number, please?
D 5546-247312
I How old are you, Diego?
D I'm forty-two.
I And … what's your job?
D I'm a taxi driver.
I And … are you married?
D No, I'm not.
I Thank you very much.

Grace Chou
I = Interviewer, G = Grace
I Good afternoon.
G Good afternoon.
I What's your name, please?
G Grace, Grace Chou.

I And where are you from?
G From New York.
I Ah! So you're from the United States.
G Yes, I am.
I What's your phone number?
G 212 638-9475
I Thank you. How old are you?
G I'm thirty-three.
I What's your job, Miss Chou?
G I'm a shop assistant.
I And are you married?
G Yes, I am.
I That's fine. Thank you very much.

T 3.9
1 The band, *Metro 5*, are in Brazil.
They aren't in Brazil! They're in the United States!
2 They're in New York.
They aren't in New York! They're in Las Vegas!
3 Bo's from Australia.
He isn't from Australia! He's from Sweden!
4 Edson's from Sweden.
He isn't from Sweden! He's from Brazil!
5 They're very tired.
They aren't tired! They're happy and excited to be here!

T 3.10 Interview with the band
I = Interviewer, R = Ronan, B = Bo, E = Edson,
D&P = Donny & Paul, All = *Metro 5*
I Hi!
All Hi!
I Now, this is your first time in Las Vegas, yes?
All Yeah. That's right. It's fantastic here! It's great!
I Good! Now, one by one. Ronan you're from Australia.
R Yes, I am.
I And how old are you, Ronan?
R I'm 24.
I OK. And Bo, you're from Brazil and Edson's from Sweden …
B No, no I'm not from Brazil, Edson's from Brazil. I'm from Sweden.
I Sorry guys. So Bo and Edson, how old are you?
E We're both 21.
B Yeah. That's right.
I OK. Now, Donny and Paul. You're brothers.
D&P Yeah, we are.
I And you're from Scotland?
D&P No, no. We aren't from Scotland. We're from Ireland.
I Ireland. Oh, yes. Sorry. How old are you both?
P I'm 22.
D And I'm 19.
I Thanks. Now, who's married in *Metro 5*.
B, E, D & P We aren't married!
R I am!
I Ah, Ronan. You're married.
R Yeah, my wife's name's Lisa. She isn't here. She's in Australia.
I Aah! Well, thank you, *Metro 5*. Welcome to Las Vegas!
All It's great to be here. Thanks!

T 3.11 Social expressions
1 A I'm sorry.
B That's OK.
2 C A coffee, please.
D That's £1.20
C Thanks very much.
3 E Excuse me! Where's the station?
F It's over there.
E Thanks a lot.
4 G Thank you very much. That's very kind.
H That's OK.
5 I Qué hora es?
J I'm sorry. I don't understand.
6 K Excuse me! Where's the town centre?
L I'm sorry. I don't know.

UNIT 4

T 4.1 see p24

T 4.2
1 Is Annie married?
Yes, she is.
2 Where's their house?
It's in London.
3 What's Annie's job?
She's a doctor.
4 Where's her hospital?
In the centre of London.
5 What's Jim's job?
He's a bank manager.
6 Are their children both at school?
No. Emma's at school. Vince is at university.

T 4.3 see p25

T 4.4
1 Annie is Jim's wife.
2 Jim is Annie's husband.
3 Emma is Annie and Jim's daughter.
4 Vince is their son.
5 Annie is Vince's mother.
6 Jim is Emma's father.
7 Emma is Vince's sister.
8 Vince is Emma's brother.
9 Annie and Jim are Emma and Vince's parents.
10 Emma and Vince are Jim and Annie's children.

T 4.5 The Taylor family
1 Come on, Emma! Time for school!
2 Mum! Where are my school books?
3 Bye, everybody! I'm off to work! Have a good day!
4 Bye, Dad! See you this evening.
5 Good morning, Mrs Clark. How are you today?

T 4.6 Elena Díaz from Chicago
Hi! My name's Elena Díaz, and I'm from the United States. This is my family. Our house is in Chicago. This is my brother. His name is Oscar, and he's 19. He's a student in college. This is my mother. Her name's Maria. She's 47, and she's a Spanish teacher. And this is my father, Alfredo. He's 52, and he's a businessman.

T 4.7
1 What's your name?
   My name's Annie.
2 What are your names?
   Our names are Emma and Vince.
3 Jean-Paul and Andre are students.
   Their school is in Paris.
4 My sister's married.
   What's her husband's name?
5 My brother's office is in New York.
   What's his job?
6 We're in our English class.
7 Mum and Dad are in Rome.
   What's the name of their hotel?

T 4.8 see p27

T 4.9 Paddy's life
1 I have a small hotel in the city of Galway.
2 My wife has a job in town.
3 We have three sons.
4 The boys have a band called *Metro 5*.
5 My sister has a big house in London.

T 4.10 Questions and answers
1 How's your mother?
   She's very well, thank you.
2 What's your sister's job?
   She's a nurse.
3 How old are your daughters?
   They're ten and thirteen.
4 Who is Pedro?
   He's a student from Madrid.
5 Where's your office?
   It's in the centre of town.
6 What's your surname?
   Smith.

T 4.11 Who is it?
1 Listen to this band! It's *Metro 5*! They're fantastic!
2 My girlfriend is from the north of England.
3 London's great! And my boyfriend's great, too!
4 Our sister's at university.
   Yeah she's at university in London.
5 I like my sister's boyfriend, he's funny.
6 Our children's school is near our house.
7 My bank is in the centre of Manchester.
8 Come on, United! Come on!
   Yes! A goal! 4 – 1 to Man United!

T 4.12 **T 4.13** see p30

T 4.14 How do you spell…?
1 What's your name?
   Annie Taylor.
   How do you spell your first name?
   A–N–N–I–E
   How do you spell your surname?
   T–A–Y–L–O–R
2 What's your name?
   Quentin Wrexham.
   How do you spell your first name?
   Q–U–E–N–T–I–N.
   How do you spell your surname?
   W–R–E–X–H–A–M.
3 What's your name?
   Takako Matsuda.
   How do you spell your first name?
   T–A–K–A–K–O.

How do you spell your surname?
M–A–T–S–U–D–A.
4 What's your name?
   Fabien Leclerc.
   How do you spell your first name?
   F–A–B–I–E–N.
   How do you spell your surname?
   L–E–C–L–E–R–C.
5 What's your name?
   Idoia Ruiz Martinez.
   How do you spell your first name?
   I–D–O–I–A.
   How do you spell your surnames?
   R–U–I–Z, then M–A–R–T–I–N–E–Z.

T 4.15 see p30

T 4.16 see p31

T 4.17 Email addresses
1 A Your email address is?
   P pambowler@btinternet.com
   A B–A …
   P No, Pam. P–A–M.
   A Ah, OK. Pam.
   P Bowler. B–O–W–L–E–R.
   A Pam … Bowler … @
   P @btinternet.com
   A @btinternet.com
   P That's it.
2 B Can you tell me your email address?
   H Yes. harrylime@hotmail.co.uk
   B harrylime … All one word …
   H @hotmail …
   B @hotmail …
   H .co.uk
   B .co.uk. Great. Thanks.
3 C What's your email address?
   P paulmartin@wannado.fr
   C paul …
   P martin. M–A–R–T–I–N.
   C paulmartin …
   P @wannado …
   C wannado …
   P .fr
   C .fr. Got it.
4 D And your email address is …?
   G glennamiles@toronto.ca
   D glennamiles …
   G @toronto …
   D @toronto …
   G .ca
   D .ca. That's lovely. Thanks a lot.

UNIT 5

T 5.1
Sports
tennis football swimming skiing

Food
Italian food Chinese food pizza
hamburger oranges ice-cream

Drinks
tea coffee Coke beer wine

T 5.2 see p32

T 5.3 see p32

T 5.4 Harvey
What do I like? Well, I like sports a lot, but not all sports. I like football – American football, of course – and I like skiing! But I don't like tennis and -erm I don't like swimming very much. And food and drink? What do I like? Well, I like hamburgers, and pizza. I like Italian food a lot. But not Chinese food, I don't like Chinese food, and I don't like tea. Tea is for the English. I'm American so I like coffee sometimes, and Coke, of course. I love Coke.

T 5.5 see p33

T 5.6 Harvey and Eva
I = Interviewer, H = Harvey, E = Eva
I Harvey and Eva. You're twins. Do you like the same things?
H Well, we really, really like pizza!
E Oh, yes! It's delicious! We have pizza a lot at home and in restaurants.
I So, do you like the same food?
E Well, we both like ice-cream.
H Mmm, it's fantastic!
E But we really don't like tea! Do we Harvey?
H No, we don't. Ugh! It's awful!
I And do you both like sports?
H Yes, we do. We like skiing.
E Yeah! We like skiing a lot. It's really exciting!
H And I love football! It's great.
E No, it isn't. It's awful!

T 5.7 see p34

T 5.8
I = Interviewer, C = Colin
1 I Hello, Colin, nice to meet you. Where do you come from?
   C I come from Scotland, from Dundee.
2 I Do you live in Dundee?
   C No, I don't. I live and work in London.
3 I Do you live with friends?
   C Yes, I do. I live with two friends.
4 I Where do you work?
   C I work in an Italian restaurant.
5 I Do you like Italian food?
   C Yes, I do. I like it a lot.
6 I Do you drink Italian wine?
   C Yes, I do. I drink wine but I don't drink beer. I don't like it.
7 I Do you like your job?
   C No, I don't. I want to be an actor.
8 I Do you speak Italian?
   C No, I don't. I speak Spanish and French, but I don't speak Italian.

T 5.9
Conversations with Colin
1 Colin Goodbye guys. Time for work.
   A   Bye. Colin. See you later.
   Colin Yeah. Very late tonight.
   A   Oh yes. It's Friday.
   Colin Yes, I work late on Fridays. Bye.
2 Colin Good evening. Do you want to order?
   B   Ah yes. We both want pizzas.
   C   Yes, two Pizza Margheritas please.
   Colin Fine. And do you want wine?

B Oh yes, we do. Do you have a wine list?

Colin Yes, of course. Here it is.

3 **D** OK, Colin and Anna come here!

Colin What do you want?

D I want you to read it again with Anna. OK? You are Romeo, Anna is Juliet of course.

Anna Fine. 'Oh Romeo, Romeo where …'

D No, no! Terrible. You love Romeo, really love him. Again.

Anna Romeo, Romeo wherefore art thou, Romeo …

4 **Mum** Hello?

Colin Hi, Mum!

Mum Oh hello Colin. Donald, It's your big brother! … Colin, how are you?

Colin I'm fine Mum, really fine.

Mum Do you like your flat?

Colin Yes, I do but it's a bit small for three people.

Mum Ah, yes. It is small. But do you like your work?

Colin No, I don't. Not really. But I like the food.

Mum Oh, yes. Italian food is good.

Colin Yeah but I like your food the best, Mum! It's delicious!

Mum Ooh, thank you Colin. Now, do you want to speak to your brother?

Colin Yes, of course. Hi Donald. It's your brother …

T 5.10 **Languages and nationalities**

England	English
Germany	German
Italy	Italian
Mexico	Mexican
Brazil	Brazilian
Japan	Japanese
Portugal	Portuguese
China	Chinese
France	French
the United States	American
Spain	Spanish

T 5.11 **What language do they speak?**

1 In Brazil they speak Portuguese.
2 In Canada they speak English and French.
3 In France they speak French.
4 In Germany they speak German.
5 In Italy they speak Italian.
6 In Japan they speak Japanese.
7 In Mexico they speak Spanish.
8 In Egypt they speak Arabic.
9 In Spain they speak Spanish.
10 In Switzerland they speak German, French, and Italian.

T 5.12 **What's this? Where's it from?**

1 It's an American car.
2 It's German beer.
3 They're Spanish oranges.
4 It's a Japanese camera.
5 It's Mexican food.
6 It's an English dictionary.
7 It's an Italian bag.
8 It's Brazilian coffee.
9 It's French wine.

T 5.13 **At a party**
F = Flavia, T = Terry

F Hello. I'm Flavia. Flavia Rossi. What's your name?

T Hi Flavia. I'm Terry. Terry Adams.

F Do you work here in London, Terry?

T Well, I work in London but I don't live in London. I live in Brighton.

F And what's your job?

T I'm an actor. What's your job, Flavia? Do you work in London?

F Yes, I do. I work in a hotel. A big hotel near here.

T Flavia, you aren't English, but you speak English very well. Where do you come from?

F I come from Italy, from Napoli. Or Naples I think you say.

T Ah, Italy. I love Italy.

F Do you know Naples?

T No, I don't. I don't know Naples, but I know Rome. I like Rome very much. It's very beautiful.

F Naples is beautiful too. Do you speak Italian, Terry?

T No, I don't. I speak French but I don't speak Italian.

F It's nice to meet you Terry.

T You too.

T 5.14 **T 5.15** **T 5.16** see p39

T 5.17 **How much is it?**

1 The cheese sandwich is £2.90.
2 The football is £14.
3 The iPhone is £90.95.
4 The beer is £3.50.
5 The dictionary is £7.50.
6 The pair of jeans is £50.
7 The chocolate is 60p.
8 The bag is £44.99.

UNIT 6

T 6.1 **The time**

1 It's nine o'clock.
2 It's nine thirty.
3 It's nine forty-five.
4 It's ten o'clock.
5 It's ten fifteen.
6 It's two o'clock.
7 It's two thirty.
8 It's two forty-five.
9 It's three o'clock.
10 It's three fifteen.

T 6.2 see p40

T 6.3 **Kim's day**

Kim Well, on schooldays I get up at seven forty-five. I have breakfast at eight and I go to school at eight thirty. I have lunch in school with my friends, that's at twelve fifteen – it's early in our school. I leave school at three thirty in the afternoon and I walk home with my friends. I get home at four thirty, have tea, and watch television. I go to bed at eleven o'clock on schooldays, but later at the weekend, of course!

T 6.4 see p41

T 6.5 **Elliot's day**

He gets up at six o'clock and has a shower. He has breakfast at six forty-five. He leaves home at seven fifteen, and he goes to work by taxi. He has lunch, a Coca Cola and a sandwich, in his office at one o'clock. He always works late. He leaves work at eight o'clock in the evening. He sometimes buys a pizza and eats it at home. He gets home at nine fifteen. He never goes out in the evening. He works at his computer until eleven thirty. He always goes to bed at eleven forty-five. He watches television in bed.

T 6.6

gets up   has   leaves   works   buys   goes   watches

T 6.7

He always works late.
He sometimes buys a pizza.
He never goes out in the evening.
He always goes to bed at eleven forty-five.

T 6.8 see p42

T 6.9 **Questions and negatives**

1 What time does he get up?
He gets up at six o'clock.
2 When does he go to bed?
He goes to bed at eleven forty-five.
3 Does he go to work by taxi?
Yes, he does.
4 Does he have lunch in a restaurant?
No, he doesn't.
5 Does he go out in the evening?
No, he doesn't.

T 6.10

1 When does he leave home?
He leaves home at 7.15.
2 Does he go to work by bus?
No, he goes to work by taxi.
3 Where does he have lunch?
He has lunch in his office.
4 Does he usually work late?
Yes, he does, every day.
5 Does he eat in a restaurant?
No, he doesn't. He eats at home.
6 What does he do in the evening?
He works. He never goes out.

T 6.11 **Lois' Day**
Lois Maddox
The seaside artist fills her day with work, walks, music, and friends.

Lois Maddox is twenty-five and she's an artist. She lives in a small house by the sea in Cape Cod, Massachusets. She always gets up late, at ten o'clock in the morning. She has a big breakfast, coffee, eggs and toast – and then she goes to the beach with her dog. When she gets home she works in her studio until seven o'clock in the evening. She never eats lunch but she always cooks a big dinner and she often invites friends. After dinner, she usually listens to music or plays the piano, sometimes she phones her brother, Elliot, in New York. She goes to bed very late, at one or two o'clock in the morning.

T 6.12　On the phone

L = Lois, E = Elliot

L　Hi Elliot, how are you?
E　I'm fine, thanks. Busy as usual.
L　Oh, you're always busy. You and your computers!
E　I know, but I love my work.
L　I love my work too, but I relax sometimes.
E　Huh! I don't know about that. You paint all day!
L　Yes, but I stop in the evening. You never stop!
E　That's not true. Hey Lois, how's your friend Nancy?
L　Nancy? She's OK. You know, Elliot, Nancy likes you. She often asks about you.
E　Mm, I like Nancy too.
L　Well, come and visit me soon. I want to cook for you and Nancy.
E　Good idea! What about next weekend? Next Sunday?
L　Yes, great! I often invite Nancy at the weekend.
E　Great. See you on Sunday. Have a good week!

T 6.13　Negatives and pronunciation

1　She lives in a flat.
　　She doesn't live in a flat! She lives in a house!
2　He gets up at ten o'clock.
　　He doesn't get up at ten o'clock! He gets up at six o'clock!
3　She's a businesswoman.
　　She isn't a businesswoman! She's an artist!
4　He goes to work by bus.
　　He doesn't go to work by bus! He goes to work by taxi!
5　She watches television in the evening.
　　She doesn't watch television in the evening! She listens to music or plays the piano!

T 6.14　Words that go together

get up early
go to bed late
listen to music
watch TV
cook dinner
work in an office
go shopping
drink coffee
eat in restaurants
have a shower
play the piano
stay at home

T 6.15　Lifestyle questionnaire

1　Do you get up early?
2　Do you have a big breakfast?
3　Do you walk to school or work?
4　Do you go to school or work by bus?
5　Do you watch TV in the evening?
6　Do you go shopping at the weekend?
7　Do you eat in restaurants?
8　Do you drink wine?
9　Do you go to bed late?

T 6.16　Days of the week

Monday
Tuesday
Wednesday
Thursday
Friday
Saturday
Sunday

UNIT 7

T 7.1　see p49

T 7.2

1　Where do you live?
　　I live in France, in Paris.
2　Who are you married to?
　　Julien Caribe. He's French.
3　What does your husband do?
　　He's a photographer.
4　When are you in Sydney again?
　　Next October.
5　Who are the kids in the photos?
　　My daughters Freya and Frida, and my son Pierre Louis.
6　How old are they?
　　They're six, four, and ten months old.
7　Why do your daughters have Swedish names?
　　Because their father is Swedish.
8　How many shows do you do every year?
　　About eight.
9　Why do you work so hard?
　　Because I love my work.
10　What do you do in your free time?
　　I go out with my family.

T 7.3

Gina is a fashion model. Paris is her favourite city. She loves it there. Next October she's in Sydney for a fashion show. She is now married to a Frenchman. They have a baby son. Friday is their favourite day.

T 7.4　*This* and *that*

1　A　This is my favourite family photo.
　　B　Ah, yes. You all look very happy!
2　C　Who's that?
　　D　The guy in the hat? That's the boss!
3　E　What's that?
　　F　It's my new MP3 player.
　　E　Wow! It's great!
4　G　How much is this?
　　H　£9.50.
　　G　I'll have it, please.
5　I　How much is that?
　　J　It's £500.
　　I　I love it. It's fantastic!
6　K　Is this your phone?
　　L　Yes, it is. Thanks.
7　M　I like that coat.
　　N　The blue one?
　　M　No, the red one!
8　O　I like this wine.
　　P　Where's it from?
　　O　Chile. It's delicious.
9　Q　This is for you.
　　P　A present? For me? Why?
　　Q　Because I love you!

T 7.5　I like them!

1　Do you like ice-cream?
　　Yes, I love it.
2　Do you like dogs?
　　No, I hate them.

3　Do you like me?
　　Of course I like you!
4　Does your teacher teach you French?
　　No, she teaches us English.
5　Do you like your teacher?
　　We like her very much.

T 7.6　Questions and answers

1　How do you come to school?
　　By bus.
2　What do you have for breakfast?
　　Toast and coffee.
3　Who's your favourite band?
　　I don't have a favourite. I like a lot.
4　Where does your father work?
　　In an office in the centre of town.
5　Why do you want to learn English?
　　Because it's an international language.
6　How much money do you have on you?
　　Not a lot. About £2.
7　What time do lessons start at your school?
　　They start at nine o'clock.
8　How many languages does your teacher speak?
　　Three.

T 7.7　Adjectives

1　A　It's so hot today, isn't it?
　　B　I know. It's 35 degrees!
2　C　Hey! I like your new shoes!
　　D　Thank you! They're really nice, aren't they?
　　C　They're fantastic!
3　E　I live in a very small flat.
　　F　How many bedrooms do you have?
　　E　Only one!
4　G　How much is that coat?
　　H　£150.
　　G　Wow! That's too expensive for me.
5　I　Your name's Peter, isn't it?
　　J　Yes, that's right.
　　I　Nice to meet you, Peter.

T 7.8　see p53

T 7.9

1　Can I have a return ticket to Oxford, please?
2　I like this jumper. Can I try it on?
3　I want to post these letters to the Czech Republic, please.
4　Can I have a coffee, please?
5　Some aspirin, please.

T 7.10

I = Iveta

1　In a railway station
　　I　Can I have a return ticket to Oxford, please?
　　A　Sure.
　　I　How much is that?
　　A　Twenty-two pounds fifty, please.
　　I　Can I pay by credit card?
　　A　No problem. Put your card in the machine. And enter your PIN number, please.

2　In a clothes shop
　　I　Hello. Can I try on this jumper, please?
　　B　Of course. The changing rooms are over there.

3 In a post office

I Can I post these letters to the Czech Republic, please?
C Sure. Put them on the scales. That's £1.68.
I Thank you. How much is a stamp for a postcard to the United States?
C Sixty-two p.
I Can I have three, please?

4 In a café

D Yes, please!
I Can I have a coffee, please? A latte.
D Large or small?
I Small please. To take away.
D Sure. Anything to eat?
I No, thank you. Just a coffee.
D Thanks a lot.

5 In a chemist's

E Next, please!
I Hello. Can I have some aspirin, please?
E Twelve or twenty-four ?
I Pardon?
E Do you want a packet of twelve aspirin or twenty-four?
I Oh, twelve's fine, thanks.

UNIT 8

T 8.1 Rooms of a house

bathroom   bedroom   kitchen
dining room   living room

T 8.2 Things in a house

a bed	an armchair
a cooker	a lamp
a sofa	a picture
a TV	a magazine
a shower	a DVD player
a toilet	a laptop
a table	a desk
a fridge	

T 8.3 Robert's living room

My living room isn't very big, but I think it's great. There's an old sofa, and there are two armchairs. There's a table with a TV and a DVD player on it.

There's also a PlayStation. I love all the games. There are some books, and there are a lot of pictures and posters on the walls. There are two lamps. My room's not very tidy but it's really comfortable.

T 8.4 see p57

T 8.5 Robert and his mum

R= Robert, M = Mum

R Hi, Mum.
M Robert. How are you? How's the new flat?
R It's great, Mum. I love it. It's really comfortable.
M And tidy?
R Er- well …
M So, tell me about it. Is there a nice sofa?
R Well, there's an old sofa but it's OK.
M Mmm. And are there any chairs?
R Yes, of course, there are chairs. There are two big armchairs.
M Good. And a TV. Is there a TV?
R Oh, yes, there is. The TV's really big. And I have a DVD player and a PlayStation and …
M A PlayStation? Why?
R Mum, I love playing games!
M OK, OK. So is there a desk?
R There isn't a desk in the living room but there's one in the bedroom.
M Good. Now, are there any pictures on the walls? Any photographs of your family?
R Well, in the living room there are my posters of New York and Sydney but there aren't any photographs, they're all in my bedroom.
M OK. Now your father and I want to see this flat. Can we visit next…?
R Visit? You want to visit?
M Yes. We're free next weekend. Can we come?
R Er- next weekend -er sorry Mum, -er I think -er …

T 8.6 Robert's bedroom

1 His laptop is on the desk.
2 The CD player is next to the laptop.
3 There are three books on the floor next to his bed.
4 His car keys are in the drawer.
5 There's a football on the floor under the desk.
6 His trainers are next to his bag under his bed.

T 8.7 Questions and answers

1 Do you live in a house or a flat?
2 How many bedrooms are there?
3 Is there a phone in the kitchen?
4 Is there a television in the living room?
5 Is there a DVD player under the television?
6 Are there a lot of books in your bedroom?
7 Are there any pictures on the wall?

T 8.8 Which room is it?

There's a cat on the sofa, and there's a phone on a small table next to the sofa. There's a CD player with some CDs under it. Not a lot of CDs. There isn't a TV, and there aren't any pictures or photographs on the walls. There's one lamp. It's next to the table with the phone. There are two tables and two armchairs. There are some books under one of the tables.

T 8.9 Vancouver – the best city in the world

Vancouver is called the 'best city in the world'. Why? Is it the spectacular mountains? The beautiful beaches? The excellent shops and restaurants? It's all of this and more!

Where is it?

Vancouver is in south-west Canada, next to the Pacific Ocean, 24 miles from the US border.

When to go

It is always a good time to visit Vancouver. The weather is never too cold or too hot. It is warm and sunny in summer but it rains a lot in autumn and winter.

What to do

In spring, go skiing in the mountains in the morning and sunbathe on the beach in the afternoon. In summer, go swimming, sailing or fishing or go walking in North America's biggest park, Stanley Park. There are excellent shops in Yaletown, and there is also theatre, opera, and music of every sort. Vancouver is the 'City of Festivals'.

Where to eat

Vancouver is a cosmopolitan city, so there are French, Italian, Japanese, Indian, Thai, and Chinese restaurants. Vancouver's Chinatown is the second biggest in North America, after San Francisco. There is also a lot of delicious, fresh seafood.

Where to stay

In the busy city centre there are some excellent, expensive hotels. The beautiful Fairmont Hotel is $400 a night, but next to the sea there are a lot of cheap, comfortable hotels from $59 a night.

How to travel

You don't need a car in Vancouver. There are slow, old trolley buses and there is the fast, modern Sky Train. Take the ferry – it is a great way to see the city.

T 8.10 My home town

Hi! My name's Steve and I live in Vancouver. I work at an international bank in the centre of the city but I live in English Bay near the beach. I have a small apartment there. Vancouver's a great city. It's really cosmopolitan. People from all over the world live here. Every Friday after work my girlfriend and I go to Chinatown and have delicious Chinese food – it's my favourite.

I like the weather because it's never too hot or too cold, but it rains a lot and I don't like that.

I work hard and I play hard! I love sport and Vancouver's good for so many sports. In winter I go skiing every weekend, I like snowboarding too. In summer I go swimming and I play golf. I often go cycling with my girlfriend. Sometimes we cycle along the Vancouver Seawall to the park – Stanley Park. The mountains look fantastic from there.

Why doesn't everyone want to live in Vancouver? It's the best place to live in the world!

T 8.11 Who is it?

Conversation 1
Steve Morning. Monday again!
A Yeah. I hate Mondays and it's another busy day.
Steve I know. I have three meetings this morning.

Conversation 2
Steve Hi, can I meet you after work?
B Yeah, that's great.
Steve Six o'clock OK? We can go to that restaurant next to the Chinese supermarket.
B Fine. I want to go there again. The food's delicious.

Conversation 3
Steve Oh no! Rain again!
C It's not so bad.
Steve Yes it is. The sky's really black.
C You're right. No golf today, then!

Conversation 4
Steve It's a lovely afternoon. Do you want to go out?
D Yeah, where do you want to go?

Steve What about Stanley Park?
D Great, I love that Park! The mountains look fantastic from there.
Steve Come on then! Let's get the bikes.

T 8.12 **Directions**

1 Go up North Road. Turn left at the bank into Charles Street. It's on the right next to the theatre.
2 Go up North Road. Turn right at the school into Hillside Road, and it's on the left next to the chemist's.
3 Go up North Road. Turn right at the church into Station Road. Go straight down, and it's on the right next to the car park.
4 Go straight on up North Road for five minutes, and it's in Albert Square. It's a big building on the right.
5 Go straight on up North Road. At the post office turn left into Park Lane. It's on the right, past the Chinese restaurant.

 UNIT 9

T 9.1 **Years**

1 nineteen ninety-six
2 nineteen sixteen
3 two thousand and two
4 seventeen ninety-nine
5 eighteen forty
6 two thousand and five

T 9.2 **see p64**

T 9.3

Jane Austen
Jane Austen, the English writer, was born in 1775, in Hampshire, in the south of England.

Luciano Pavarotti
Luciano Pavarotti, the Italian opera singer, was born in 1935, in Modena, in the north of Italy.

T 9.4 **see p64**

T 9.5 **see p65**

T 9.6 **Magalie Dromard**
My name's Magalie. It's a French name, but I'm not French. I'm English. I was born in 1994. I have two brothers and a sister. My eldest brother's a doctor. His name's Tristan, and he was born in 1985. My sister is also older than me. Her name's Cecilia and she's a teacher, and she was born in 1988. And my little brother is Matt, and he was born in 1996. He's still a student. My father is French. His name's André, he's from Marseille, and he was born in, I think …1958. My mother is English, her name's Ella, she's from Manchester, and she was born in, er … 1961. My grandmother, who is my mother's mother, is called Edith. Isn't that a lovely name? She was born in Bristol in … I'm not sure, but I think about 1935.

T 9.7 **When were they born?**
1 Shakespeare was born in 1564 in Stratford-upon-Avon, England.
2 Mozart was born in Salzburg, Austria, in 1756.

3 Diana Spencer was born in Sandringham, England, in 1961.
4 Andy Warhol was born in 1928 in Pittsburgh, in the United States.
5 Michael Jackson was born in 1958 in Indiana, in the United States.
7 Marilyn Monroe was born in 1926 in Los Angeles, in the United States.
8 Ayrton Senna was born in 1960 in São Paulo, Brazil.

T 9.8 **see p66**

T 9.9 **see p67**

T 9.10
1 A Ayrton Senna was an actor.
  B No, he wasn't! He was a racing driver!
2 A Jane Austen was a princess.
  B No, she wasn't! She was a writer!
3 A Marilyn Monroe and Michael Jackson were Italian.
  B No, they weren't! They were American!
4 A Mozart was a scientist.
  B No, he wasn't! He was a musician!
5 A Luciano Pavarotti and Michael Jackson were politicians.
  B No, they weren't! They were singers!
6 A Benazir Bhutto was a writer.
  B No, she wasn't! She was a politician!

T 9.11

go	went
come	came
have	had
be	was
make	made
see	saw
buy	bought
say	said
find	found

T 9.12 **Who is Jackson Pollock?**
Teri Horton, a 60-year-old lady from Los Angeles, went shopping in San Bernardino, a town in California, USA. She was in a charity shop when she saw a colourful, modern painting. She bought it for $5.

An art teacher saw the painting and said it was by the American artist, Jackson Pollock. 'Who is Jackson Pollock?' said Teri. She had no idea that he was a very famous modern painter. Many art experts came to her house to see the painting. Some said that it wasn't a 'Pollock', but one expert, Peter Paul Biró, found Pollock's fingerprint on the back. Biró said, 'This is a real Pollock painting'.

A rich businessman was happy to pay $9 million for it, but Teri said: 'No! I want $50 million.'

In 2007, a Canadian TV company made a film about Teri and the painting. It is now for sale in an art gallery in Toronto. Price: $50 million!

T 9.13
1 Yesterday I met my mother at one o'clock and we had lunch in a restaurant.
2 I hate doing housework but last Sunday I did a lot because my house was a mess.

3 Yesterday was a lovely day so I went for a walk in the park.
4 Usually I walk but yesterday I went to work by bus.
5 On Saturday night I went to a great party. I had a really good time.
6 I did a lot of exercise yesterday. I went to the gym.
7 The party wasn't very good so we went home early.

T 9.14 **Months of the year**
January February March April May June July August September October November December

T 9.15 **T 9.16** **see p71**

T 9.17
the first of January
the third of March
the seventh of April
the twentieth of May
the second of June
the twelfth of August
the fifteenth of November
the thirty-first of December

T 9.18 **Happy Birthday!**
Happy Birthday to you!
Happy Birthday to you!
Happy Birthday, dear Sarah!
Happy Birthday to you!
Hip hip! Hooray!

 UNIT 10

T 10.1 **Angie's weekend**
Yesterday was Sunday, so I got up late, about 11.30. I had a big breakfast, orange juice, toast, eggs, and coffee. Then I went shopping, just to the supermarket, and I bought some tea, some milk, and the Sunday papers. Then I just stayed at home for the rest of the day. In the morning I cleaned my flat and in the afternoon I did some work on my computer for a bit, then in the evening I watched a film on TV. I went to bed early, about 11.00. I was tired. I had a late night on Saturday.

T 10.2 **Regular verbs**

/t/	cooked
	watched
/d/	played
	listened
/ɪd/	started
	wanted

T 10.3

A = Angie, R = Rick
A Hi, Rick. Did you have a good weekend?
R Yes, I did, thanks.
A What did you do yesterday?
R Well, I got up early and I played tennis with some friends.
A You got up early on Sunday!
R Well, yes, it was such a lovely day.
A Where did you play tennis?
R In the park. We had lunch in the café there.

A Oh, great! Did you go out in the evening?
R No, I didn't. I cooked a meal for my sister.
A Mmm! What did you have?
R Roast beef. It was delicious! What about you Angie? Did you have a good weekend?

T 10.4 p73

T 10.5 Angie's weekend
A = Angie, R = Rick
R What about you Angie? Did you have a good weekend?
A Oh yes, I did, very good.
R What did you do on Saturday?
A Well, on Saturday morning I went shopping. Then on Saturday evening I went to a party. It was great!
R Who did you see at the party?
A Oh, one or two old friends.
R Did you go out on Sunday?
A Oh no, I didn't. I didn't go out because I was too tired. I stayed at home most of the day.
R Did you do anything on Sunday evening?
A No, I didn't do much. I just watched a film on TV. I didn't go to bed late. About 11.00.

T 10.6 see p73

T 10.7 Making conversation
1 I went shopping yesterday.
  Really? What did you buy?
2 We went to that new Italian restaurant last night.
  Mmm! What did you have?
3 We saw a lot of our friends in the coffee bar.
  Oh! Who did you see?
4 I played tennis at the weekend.
  Oh, really? Where did you play?
5 The party on Saturday was great!
  Oh, good! What time did you leave?

T 10.8 Making conversation
1 **A** I went shopping yesterday.
  B Really? Where did you go?
  A Oxford Street.
  B Oh! What did you buy?
  A Well, I wanted a new coat, and I went into Selfridges.
  B Did you find one?
  A Yes, I did. I found a beautiful black one. It was only £50!
2 **A** Tom and I went to that new Italian restaurant last night.
  B Mmm! What did you have?
  A Well, I had pasta and Tom had pizza.
  B Did you enjoy it?
  A Very much. And it wasn't expensive.
3 **A** We saw a lot of our friends in the coffee bar.
  B Oh! Who did you see?
  A Angie and Rick and some other friends from work.
  B I don't think I know them.
  A They're very nice.
4 **A** I played tennis at the weekend.
  B Oh, really? Where did you play?
  A In the park. It was lovely. It was so sunny.
  B What a great thing to do on a Sunday morning!

5 **A** The party on Saturday was great!
  B Oh, good! What time did you leave?
  A Three in the morning. The music was fantastic!
  B Did you dance?
  A Of course! All night!

T 10.9 Jack and Millie's holiday
J = Jack, M = Millie
J Well, we usually go on holiday in summer …
M Yes, usually we go to Italy for our holidays, don't we?
J But last year we did something different. We had a holiday in winter, and we went to Colorado, in America.
M Because we wanted to learn to ski, you see, and we wanted a change. In Italy we always stay in a villa …
J … but in Aspen, Colorado we stayed in a very nice hotel, and because we were in a hotel, we had all our meals in restaurants.
M And that's very special for us. In Italy we cook at home in the villa. But in Colorado we went to a different restaurant every night!
J In Italy, because it's summer and it's hot, we go swimming in the swimming pool, and sit in the sun, and I play tennis sometimes …
M Jack loves his tennis, don't you darling?
J I do, but of course last year in Colorado we learned to ski, so we went skiing every day. And Millie, you went ice-skating, didn't you?
M We both went ice-skating!
J That's right! It was great fun! In Italy in the evening, we usually play cards or read …
M … but last year in Colorado we went out every night, and we met lots of lovely people, didn't we?
J We did. We had a really good time.
M And we have a good time in Italy, too, don't we?
J Mmm, we're very lucky.

T 10.10
1 Last year Jack and Millie didn't go on holiday in summer. They went in winter.
2 They didn't go to Italy. They went to Colorado.
3 They stayed in a hotel. They didn't stay in a villa.
4 They didn't eat at home. They ate in restaurants.
5 They went skiing. They didn't go swimming.

T 10.11
1 **A** Hello. Can I help you?
  B Yes. Can I have a map of the city, please?
  A Of course. Here you are.
  B Can you show me where we are on the map?
  A Yes. We're here in Regent Street in the city centre.
2 **C** We want to go on a bus tour of the city.
  A That's fine. The next bus leaves at 10.00. It takes about an hour and a half.
  C Where does the bus go from?
  A It goes from Trafalgar Square, but you can get on and off when you want.

3 **D** I want to visit the British Museum. What time does it open?
  A It opens at 10.00 in the morning and closes at 5.30 in the evening.
  D How much is it to get in?
  A It's free!

UNIT 11

T 11.1
1 Marcus is an interpreter. He can speak French and German fluently.
2 Laura is an architect. She can draw well.
3 Justin is a pilot. He can fly 747 jumbo jets.
4 George is a farmer. He can drive a tractor.
5 Lola is an athlete. She can run very fast.
6 Oliver is a schoolboy. He can use a computer really well.
7 Margaret is Oliver's grandmother. She can make fantastic cakes.

T 11.2 **T 11.3** see p81

T 11.4 Of course I can!
D = Dominique, O = Oliver
D Can you use a computer, Oliver?
O Yes, of course I can. All my friends can. I use a computer at home in my bedroom and we use computers at school all the time.
D That's great. What other things can you do?
O Well, I can run fast, very fast, and I can draw a bit. I can draw really good cars but I can't drive them of course! I can draw good planes, too. When I'm big I want to be a pilot and fly 747s.
D Excellent. Now, I know you can speak French.
O Yes, I can. I can speak French fluently because my dad's French. We sometimes speak French at home.
D Can you speak any other languages?
O No, I can't. I can't speak German or Spanish, just French – and English of course! And I can cook! I can make cakes. My grandma makes fantastic cakes and I sometimes help her. Yesterday we made a big chocolate cake!

T 11.5 Pronunciation
1 I can ski quite well.
2 She can't speak German at all.
3 He can speak English fluently.
4 Why can't you come to my party?
5 We can't understand our teacher.
6 They can read music.
7 Can I have an ice-cream, please?
8 Can cats swim?

T 11.6 Jenni Spitzer
I live in the city of Tucumán. I teach English. I can speak Spanish fluently and German a little bit.

I love it here. Saturday night is dancing night and I go dancing with friends. A lot of my friends can play the guitar really well. I can't play a musical instrument but I can dance very well. I love the music. On Sundays I often go riding here. I can ride quite well now. Or sometimes I watch friends playing golf. I can't play golf but I like watching it. Sunday is also the day for 'asado' or barbecues. We always cook beef, I can't cook at all but I want to learn. It's a great life here, everyone is really friendly.

T 11.7 **Requests and offers**

1 A Can I help you?
  B Yes, please. I want to buy this postcard.
2 A Can you tell me the time, please?
  B It's about three thirty.
3 A Can you come to my party?
  B Sorry. I can't. It's my grandma's birthday on Saturday.
4 A Can I have a glass of water, please?
  B Yes, of course. Here you are.
5 A Can you speak more slowly, please?
  B I'm sorry. Is this better? Can you understand me now?
6 A Can I give you a lift?
  B Oh, yes please! That's so kind of you!

T 11.8 **see p84**

T 11.9 **What do you do on the Internet?**

1 **Charlotte, age 14**
  I use the Internet a lot. Every day, I think. It helps me with my homework. I 'google' for information or I use *Wikipedia*. It helps me with everything, history, geography, science, English -er everything. Yesterday I got a lot information about Jane Austen.

2 **Lauren, age 20**
  I go on *Facebook* a lot, sometimes three or four times a day. It's a great way to hear all your friends' news and see all their photographs. Yesterday I posted all the photos from my party last weekend. You can see them if you want.

3 **Santiago, age 23**
  I play the guitar and I can find lots of songs on the Internet. Yesterday I got the words and music for *Can't buy me love*, you know, by the Beatles. I can play it now. I use the Internet mostly in the evenings, when I have time.

4 **Alan Krum, age 47**
  Well, my surname, -er my family name is Krum and I want to write about my family, so I use the Internet to find out about my family's history. There are special websites for this. Also, I can chat to people with the same name from all over the world, Canada, Germany, Argentina. It's really interesting. I usually use it on Sundays because I have more time then.

5 **Max, age 10**
  I play games a lot. And I go on websites for my favourite pop groups and football players. I want to be on the computer all the time, but my mum says I can't. She says I can only use it after school for an hour, and then I stop.

6 **Edna, age 71**
  I go shopping on the Internet. Every Friday I go to my son's house and I use his computer. It's fantastic – the supermarket brings all my shopping to my home. I want a computer now. I want to send emails to my friends. Most of my friends have computers.

T 11.10 **Adjectives and nouns**

1 A A Ferrari is a fantastic car. It's so fast.
  B Yeah, I know, but it's also so expensive.
2 A How tall is your brother?
  B He's very tall, 1.9 metres. I'm only 1.7 metres.
3 A I think motor racing is a really dangerous sport.
  B I know it's dangerous but it's exciting too. That's why I love it!
4 A Can I have a fresh orange juice, please?
  B I'm afraid we don't have fresh.
  A OK. Just a glass of water then.
5 A New York is a very cosmopolitan city. I love it.
  B Me too. I can't believe I'm here.
6 A Charlie Chaplin made some very funny films, don't you think?
  B No. I don't like his films. I think they're really boring.
7 A We can't go for a walk, it's too cold and wet.
  B Yes, we can. Look it's sunny again! Come on!

T 11.11 **Everyday problems**

1 A Excuse me! Can you help me? I'm lost.
  B Where do you want to go?
  A Grand Central Station.
  B Turn left onto Park Avenue. It's straight on. You can't miss it.
2 A Oh, no!
  B What's the matter?
  A There's something wrong with my computer. I can't get on the Internet, so I can't send my emails.
  B Turn everything off and try again. That sometimes works.
3 A Excuse me! This ticket machine doesn't work.
  B Did you push the green button?
  A Oh! No, I didn't.
  B Ah, well. Here's your ticket.
  A Thank you very much.
4 A Come on! It's time to go to the airport.
  B But I can't find my passport! I can't find it anywhere!
  A You put it in your bag.
  B Did I? Oh, yes. Here it is! Phew!
5 A Are you all right?
  B Yes, I think so.
  A Does your arm hurt?
  B It hurts a bit, but I think it's OK.
6 A I'm so sorry I'm late.
  B It's OK. The film starts in 15 minutes.
  A I missed the bus.
  B I told you, it doesn't matter. Come on! Let's go.

UNIT 12

T 12.1 **What can you do where?**

1 You can buy a magazine in a newsagent's.
2 You can buy bread, milk, fruit, and meat in a supermarket.
3 You can get US dollars from a bank.
4 You can buy stamps and send a parcel in a post office.
5 You can buy a dictionary in a bookshop.
6 You can get a medium latte in a coffee shop.
7 You can buy shampoo and conditioner in a chemist's.

T 12.2 **Saying what you want**

1 Adam Good morning. I'd like some ham, please.
  B How much would you like?
  Adam Four slices.
  B Would you like anything else?
  Adam Yes, I'd like some cheese. Do you have any Emmental?
  B I'm afraid we don't have any Emmental. What about Gruyère?
  Adam No, thank you. Just the ham then. How much is that?
2 C Can I help you?
  Adam Yes, please, I'd like some shampoo.
  C We have lots. Would you like it for dry or normal hair?
  Adam Dry, I think.
  C OK. Try this one. Anything else?
  Adam Er- oh yeah. I don't have any conditioner. I'd like some conditioner for dry hair, please.
  C Yes, of course. That's £6.90 please.

T 12.3 **Where is Adam?**

1 D Is that all? *The Times* and the two magazines?
  Adam Yes, that's all. Oh, I nearly forgot – I'd like some stamps, too.
  D First or second class?
  Adam First. Two books of first class stamps, please.
  D OK. Would you like a bag?
  Adam No, thanks. I don't need a bag.
  D That's £9.65.
2 Adam I'd like a latte, please.
  E Drink here or take away?
  Adam To drink here, please.
  E Small, medium or large?
  Adam Medium, please.
  E Would you like something to eat?
  Adam Er – yes. I'd like some chocolate cake.
  E Sure. Anything else?
  Adam That's it, thanks.

T 12.4 **Lily and Adam**

A= Adam, L = Lily

A What would you like to drink?
L A juice. I'd like an apple juice, please.
A Er … I have some orange juice, but I don't have any apple juice.
L Don't worry. Orange juice is fine. Thanks.
A Would you like something to eat?

L   Yeah, OK. A sandwich. A cheese sandwich?
A   Er … I don't have any cheese. Sorry. I have some ham. Would you like a ham sandwich?
L   I don't like ham.
A   Would you like some cake, then?
L   Yes, please. I'd love some.

T 12.5 It's my birthday!

A   Hey, isn't it your birthday soon?
B   Yeah, next week on the 15th.
A   So, what would you like for your birthday?
B   I don't know. I don't need anything.
A   But, I'd like to buy you something.
B   That's kind but I think I'd like to forget my birthday this year.
A   What? You don't want any presents! Why not?
B   Well, I'm 30 next week and that feels old.
A   30 isn't old. Come on. I'd like to take you out for a meal with some friends. You can choose the restaurant.
B   OK, then. Thank you. I'd like that. Just don't tell anyone it's my birthday.
A   Oh, that's silly!

T 12.6 Birthday wishes

Kelly   What would I like for my birthday? That's easy! I'd like to have breakfast in bed. With the newspapers. And in the evening I'd like to go to the theatre.

Mike   Well, I'd like a new computer, because my computer is so old that new programs don't work on it. And then in the evening I'd like to go to a good restaurant. I don't mind if it's Italian, French, Chinese or English. Just good food.

Jade   I'd love a new mobile phone. My mobile is so old now. I'd like one that takes good photos, your phone has a really good camera and it wasn't that expensive. And in the evening I'd like to go out with all my friends and have a great time!

T 12.7 see p91

T 12.8 Listening and pronunciation

1 A What would you like? Would you like a Coke?
   B Yes, please. I'm very thirsty.
2 A What sort of thing do you like doing at the weekend?
   B Well, I like watching films.
3 A What sort of flat do you want to move into?
   B Well …
   C We'd like a flat with two bedrooms. Somewhere near the centre.
4 A We have this weekend free. What would you like to do?
   B I'd like to have the weekend with you, and only you!
   A Oooh!
5 A What do you spend all your money on?
   B Well, I like new clothes. I buy new clothes every week.

T 12.9 In a restaurant

W = Waiter, L = Liam, M = Maddy

W Are you ready to order?
L Well, I am. Are you ready Maddy?
M Yes, I am. What's the soup of the day?
W French onion soup.
M Lovely. I'd like the French onion soup to start, please.
W And to follow?
M I'd like the salmon salad with some chips on the side.
W Thank you. And you sir? What would you like?
L Er – I'd like the tomato and mozzarella salad, followed by the hamburger and chips.
W Would you like any side orders?
L No, thank you. Just the hamburger.
W And to drink?
M Sparkling water for me please. What about you Liam?
L The same for me. We'd like a bottle of sparkling water, please.
W Fine. I'll bring the drinks immediately.

T 12.10 Signs all around

1 Hey, look! That lovely red jumper is only £19.99 now.
2 Oh, no. I put my money in before I saw the sign.
3 Can you tell me where the toilets are, please?
4 This is our table. It has our name on it.
5 I'm not waiting. There are so many people.
6 Which floor is our room on? Is it the 6th or 7th?
7 Oh, dear we're too late. It doesn't open again until Monday now.
8 I'm sorry, but you can't walk here. Didn't you see the sign on the gate?

UNIT 13

T 13.1 Clothes

1	a jumper	7	trainers
2	a shirt and tie	8	a jacket
3	a T-shirt and shorts	9	a scarf
4	a skirt	10	boots
5	a dress	11	a suit
6	shoes and socks	12	trousers

T 13.2 What are they wearing?

1 Nigel's wearing a grey suit and a white shirt. He's reading his emails.
2 Lily's wearing a yellow T-shirt and white trainers. She's running.
3 Rick's wearing blue jeans and a red jumper. He's playing the guitar.
4 Eva's wearing a green jacket and brown boots. She's carrying a black bag.
5 Polly and Penny are wearing yellow dresses and blue shoes. They're eating ice-cream.

T 13.3 see p97

T 13.4 Asking questions

1 What's he doing?
   He's cooking dinner for friends.
2 What's he doing?
   He's driving to London.

3 What's he doing?
   He's having a shower after work.
4 What's she doing?
   She's writing an email to her mother.
5 What's she doing?
   She's skiing in France.
6 What's she doing?
   She's eating a strawberry ice-cream.
7 What are they doing?
   They're running fast.
8 What are they doing?
   They're dancing at a party.
9 What are they doing?
   They're playing golf in the rain.

T 13.5 Nigel at work

Nigel is a businessman. He works from 9 o'clock to 5.30 every day. He always wears a suit and tie for work. He usually has lunch at his desk at one o'clock. He arrives home at about seven o'clock every evening and he reads to his children before they go to bed. He often feels very tired at the end of the day.

T 13.6 see p99

T 13.7 Questions about Nigel

1 Are they having a good time?
   Yes, they are.
2 Where are they staying?
   They're staying in a house with a swimming pool near the beach.
3 What are the children doing?
   They're swimming in the pool.
4 What's Karen doing?
   She's sunbathing.
5 What's Nigel doing?
   He's talking on the phone.
6 Is he wearing a suit?
   No, he isn't.
7 Why is Bill calling?
   Because he has a problem.

T 13.8 This week is different

C= Colin, R = Roger, M = Margaret,
CW = Colin's wife, CS = Colin's sons,
B = boys in the hostel

Conversation 1
C   Hello, I'm Colin.
R   Hi, Colin. Lovely to meet you. This is my wife Margaret.
M   It's very good of you to come and help us.
C   I'm pleased to be here.

Conversation 2
C   That's much better. Now, read it again.
B   *There was a man who work –ed, worked hard and his busi- busi*
C   *Business*
B   *… his business became very suc – suc – cess – ful, successful!*
C   Great. You're doing well.

Conversation 3
C   Hello, darling.
CW Colin! How are you? We're all missing you.
C   I'm missing you too but I'm having a good time. It's very interesting here. Roger and Margaret are wonderful people.

Conversation 4

C   Hi, boys!
CS   Dad! Hi! We're doing our homework.
C   Hey, that's good. I'm working hard too.
CS   Are you having a good time?
C   I am. I'm with some really interesting people.
CS   Can we meet them?
C   Yes, you can. I'd like you to meet them.
CS   See you soon, Dad.
C   Yeah, can't wait! See you soon!

T 13.9   Opposite verbs

1   Please don't ask me any more questions, I can't answer them.
2   I'm selling my old car, and I'm buying a new one!
3   We always get up at seven in the morning and go to bed at eleven at night.
4   It was cold, so Tom took off his T-shirt and put on a warm jumper.
5   I usually walk to school but yesterday I was late so I ran all the way.
6   John's playing tennis with Peter today. He always loses. He never wins.
7   Don't turn off the TV, I'm watching it! Please turn it on again!

T 13.10

1   A   Would you like an espresso?
    B   No, thank you, I hate black coffee.
    A   Do you? I love it.
2   C   What time does the film start?
    D   6.45.
    C   And do you know when it finishes?
    D   About 8.30, I think.
3   E   Would you like to play tennis after work?
    F   Sorry, I can't. I'm working late again.
4   G   Our train leaves London at 13.55.
    H   And what time does it arrive in Paris?
    G   16.05.
    H   Wow! That's fast.
5   I   Did you remember to bring your dictionary?
    J   Oh, sorry. I forgot it.
    I   Not again!
6   K   Can I open the window? I'm hot.
    L   Of course. Just remember to close it when you leave the room.

T 13.11   What's the matter?

1   She's cold.   6   She's bored.
2   He's hungry.   7   He's angry.
3   They're tired.   8   She's worried.
4   He's thirsty.   9   He has a headache.
5   They're hot.   10   She has a cold.

T 13.12   Why don't you…?

1   A   What's the matter?
    B   I'm tired and thirsty.
    A   Why don't you have a cup of tea?
    B   That's a good idea.
    A   Sit down. I'll make it for you.
2   C   What's the matter?
    D   I have a bad headache.
    C   Oh dear! Why don't you take some aspirin?
    D   I don't have any.
    C   It's OK. I have some.

UNIT 14

T 14.1   Bill and Gloria's holiday

1   On Sunday they're flying to London.
2   On Monday they're going to have a bus tour of London.
3   On Tuesday they're travelling through Belgium and into Germany.
4   On Wednesday they're going to drive down the 'Romantic Road' to the Alps and Austria.
5   On Thursday they're going to drive over the Europa Bridge.
6   On Friday they're going to stop in Verona. They're going to see Juliet's balcony.
7   On Saturday evening they're having dinner in a bistro in Paris.
8   On Sunday morning they're going to the Louvre to see the Mona Lisa. In the evening, they're flying back to the US.

T 14.2   see p105

T 14.3

1   What are they doing on Tuesday?
2   What are they going to do on Wednesday?
3   When are they going to drive over the Europa Bridge?
4   What are they going to do in Verona?
5   Where are they having dinner on Saturday?
6   When are they going to the Louvre?
7   When are they flying back to the US?

T 14.4   Eddie's plans

F = Friend, E = Eddie

F   What are you doing?
E   I'm planning my holiday.
F   Oh, where are you going?
E   I'm going to South Africa. It's my first time.
F   Oh you're so lucky! When are you leaving?
E   I'm leaving next Monday morning.
F   Who are you going with?
E   I'm not going with anyone. Just me and my rucksack.
F   Where are you going to stay?
E   Well, I'm staying with friends in Cape Town. Then I'm going on safari. I'm going to sleep in a tent.
F   Fantastic! And how are you going to travel?
E   By plane to Cape Town, of course, and then by jeep when I'm on safari.
F   By jeep! How exciting. And how long are you going to stay?
E   Just two weeks. I'd like to stay longer but I can't. It's too expensive.
F   How much is it going to cost?
E   About £2,000.
F   Mmmm, that's quite a lot. Well, have a great time. I can't wait to see your photos.
E   Oh, yes, I'm going to take a lot of photos.

T 14.5   Pronunciation

Two syllables

pilot   hotel
women   arrive
married   shampoo
chocolate   enjoy

T 14.6   Pronunciation

Three syllables

photograph   banana
vegetable   magazine
interesting   understand
designer   souvenir
assistant

T 14.7   Rhymes

1   some   home   come
2   goes   knows   does
3   were   here   her
4   make   steak   speak
5   near   wear   there
6   eat   great   wait

T 14.8   Past, Present, and Future

Milena Dušek   My parents are divorced. My father is a journalist, and works for a newspaper called Blesk. My mother works as a chef in a restaurant in the Old Town. I see my father quite often. He lives nearby.

Georg Reinhardt   I was born in Frankfurt, where I grew up and went to school. I studied architecture at the University of Munich. I met Karlotta at university – she was a student of modern languages. We moved to Berlin in 1995.

Archie McCrae   I went to Drumchapel High School. I studied biology, chemistry, and physics. At school I met Fiona, and we started going out when we were 16. We studied medicine together at the University of Edinburgh, and we now live in Edinburgh.

T 14.9

Social expressions 2

1   A   Good luck in the exam! I hope it goes well.
    B   Thanks. I'll do my best.
    A   See you later. Bye!
2   C   Oh, no!
    D   Don't worry. It doesn't matter.
    C   I'm so sorry!
3   E   Have a good weekend!
    F   Thanks! Same to you! What are you doing? Anything special?
    E   We're going to a birthday party.
    F   Oh, lovely!
4   G   Goodbye! Drive carefully!
    H   Thanks! I'll phone you when I arrive.
    G   See you again soon!
5   I   I have a present for you.
    J   For me? Why?
    I   It's just to say thank-you.
    J   That's so kind of you!
6   K   Bye! And thanks for everything!
    L   It was a pleasure. We enjoyed having you.

Grammar Reference

UNIT 1

 1.1 *am/are/is*

I	'm am	Ben.
You	're are	Mika.
My name	's is	James Bond.
This	is	Judy Koblenz.

 1.2 Questions with question words

What's your name?
(what's = what is)

How are you?

 1.3 Possessive adjectives

My name's John.
What's **your** name?

1.4 Plural nouns

1 Most nouns add *-s*.
book	→	*books*
computer	→	*computers*
camera	→	*cameras*

2 Some nouns add *-es*.
sandwich	→	*sandwiches*
bus	→	*buses*

UNIT 2

2.1 *am/are/is*

I'm (am)	from England. a student.
You're (are)	
He's (is) She's (is)	
It's (is)	a computer.
They're (are)	in New York. married.

2.2 Possessive adjectives

His name's Pablo.
What's **her** name?

My name's Mika.
What's **your** name?

🛈 *his* = possessive adjective
his name, **his** car, **his** camera

He's Bruno. **He's** from Brazil. **He's** fine.
(he's = he is)

2.3 Questions with question words

Where	are you is she is he	from?
What	's your (is your) 's her (is her)	name?

2.4 *am/are/is*

I'm (am)	from England. a student. fine. in Paris. in New York. married.
You're (are)	
He's She's (is) It's	
They're (are)	

UNIT 3

▶ 3.1 am/are/is

Negative

I	'm not (am not)	a teacher.
He She	isn't (is not)	from Spain. married. very well.

Yes/No **questions and short answers**

Are you married?	Yes, I am. No, I'm not.
Is she a teacher?	Yes, she is. No, she isn't.
Is he English?	Yes, he is. No, he isn't.
Is her name Alice?	Yes, it is. No, it isn't.

▶ 3.2 Verb *to be*

Positive

I	'm (am)	
He She It	's (is)	from the US.
You We They	're (are)	

Negative

I	'm not	
He She It	isn't	English.
You We They	aren't	

Questions with question words

What	is your name? is her address? is his phone number?
Where	are you from? is he from? are they from?
How old	are you? are they?

Answers

John Mason.
16, Albert Road, Bristol.
01693 456729.

From Spain.

I'm 16.
They're 8 and 10.

Yes/No **questions**

Is	he she it	American?
Are	you we they	married?

Short answers

Yes, he is.
No, she isn't.
Yes, it is.

Yes, I am.
No, we aren't.
No, they aren't.

UNIT 4

▶ 4.1 Possessive adjectives

This is	my your his her our their	family. school. office.

▶ 4.2 Possessive *'s*

's shows possession.

This is John. This is his son. → This is John's son.
This is Marie. This is her car. → This is Marie's car.

his house → Tom's house
her name → your wife's name

🛈 *'s* is also the short form of *is*.

he's	=	he **is**
she's	=	she **is**
it's	=	it **is**
Who's	=	Who **is**

▶ 4.3 Plural nouns

1 Most nouns add *-s* in the plural.

doctor	→	doctors
book	→	books
student	→	students

2 Nouns that end in *-s*, *-ss*, *-sh*, or *-ch* add *-es*.

bus	→	buses
class	→	classes
sandwich	→	sandwiches

3 Some nouns that end in *-y* change to *-ies*.

city	→	cities
country	→	countries
dictionary	→	dictionaries

4 Some nouns are irregular.

man	→	**men**
woman	→	**women**
child	→	**children**

▶ 4.4 have/has

Have is an irregular verb.

I You We They	have	a good job. a computer.
He She It	has	

UNIT 5

5.1 Present Simple: *I/you/we/they*

Positive

I You We They	like coffee. play tennis. live in London. speak two languages. have a good job.

Negative

I You We They	don't	like tennis. speak French. work in a restaurant.

Questions with question words

Where		you live?
What sports	do	we like?
How many languages		they speak?

Yes/No questions and short answers

Do you like football?	Yes, I do. No, I don't.
Do they speak English?	Yes, they do. No, they don't.

❗ *Do you like tea?*　　*Yes, I do.*　NOT　~~*Yes, I like.*~~

5.2 *a/an*

We use *an* before words that begin with *a, e, i, o,* and *u*.
>*an actor*
>*an English dictionary*
>*an ice-cream*
>*an orange*
>*an umbrella*

but
>*a car*
>*a hamburger*
>*a television*

5.3 Adjective + noun

Adjectives always come *before* the noun.
>*an American car*　　　　　~~*a car American*~~
>*a Japanese camera*　NOT　~~*a camera Japanese*~~
>*a beautiful girl*　　　　　~~*a girl beautiful*~~

❗ *Spanish oranges*　NOT　~~*Spanishes oranges*~~

UNIT 6

6.1 Present Simple: *he/she/it*

Positive

He She	gets up	at 8.00.
It	leaves	

6.2 Spelling – Present Simple: *he/she/it*

1 Most verbs add *-s*.

he/she/it	*listens* *leaves* *walks*

2 Verbs ending in *-s, -ss, -sh, -ch* add *-es*.

he/she/it	*watches* *washes*

❗ *go, have,* and *do* are irregular.

he/she/it	**does** **goes** **has**

6.3 Adverbs of frequency

0%	40%	90%	100%
never	sometimes	usually	always

Adverbs of frequency (*never, sometimes, usually, always*) can come before the verb.
>*We **never** watch TV.*
>*She **sometimes** goes out on a Saturday night.*
>*He **usually** works late.*
>*I **always** have tea for breakfast.*

6.4 Present Simple: *he/she/it*

Negative

She He	doesn't	go out in the evening. eat in a restaurant.

Questions with question words

What		he have for lunch?
Where		she work?
What time	does	he go to bed?
When		he leave work?

Yes/No questions and short answers

Does he like football?	Yes, he does. No, he doesn't.
Does she speak English?	Yes, she does. No, she doesn't.

❗ *Does he like tea?*　　*Yes, he does.*　NOT　~~*Yes, he likes.*~~
　Do you like coffee?　*No, I don't.*　NOT　~~*No, I don't like.*~~

UNIT 7

 7.1 Question words

Look at the question words and the answers.

What?	*A hamburger.*	**How?**	*By taxi.*
When?	*In the evening.*	**How old?**	*16.*
What time?	*At 8.00.*	**How many?**	*Two.*
Who?	*Peter.*	**How much?**	*$2.*
Where?	*In Paris.*	**Why?**	*Because …*

 7.2 Pronouns

Look at the subject and object pronouns, and the possessive adjectives.

Subject pronouns	I	you	he	she	it	we	they
Object pronouns	me	you	him	her	it	us	them
Possessive adjectives	my	your	his	her	its	our	their

 7.3 *this / that*

We use *this* to refer to things near to us.

This is my son.

*I like **this** sandwich.*

We use *that* to refer to things that are not near to us.

That's my house.

*I don't like **that** car.*

UNIT 8

8.1 *There is / There are*

Positive
***There's** a sofa in the living room.*
(There's = There is)

***There are** two CD players in my house.*

Negative
***There isn't** a TV.*
***There aren't** any photos.*

Question
***Is there** a TV in the kitchen?*
***Are there** any magazines on the table?*
*How many CDs **are there**?*

8.2 *some* and *any*

We use *some* in positive sentences.
    *There are **some** books.*

We use *any* in questions and negatives.
    *Does he have **any** photographs?*
    *There aren't **any** lamps.*

See 12.2 p128 for information on *some* and *any*.

UNIT 9

9.1 was/were

Was and were are the past tense of am/are/is.

Present

I	am	
He/She It	is	fine. in class.
You We They	are	

Past

I He/She It	was	fine.
You We They	were	at home.

Negative

I He	wasn't	at home last weekend. at school yesterday.
You They	weren't	

Questions

Where **were you** yesterday?
Was she at school? Yes, **she was.**/No, **she wasn't.**

❶ We use was/were with born, not am/is/are.
Where **were** you **born**?   NOT   ~~Where are you born?~~
He **was born** in Russia.   ~~He is born in Russia.~~

9.2 Past Simple – irregular verbs

Many common verbs are irregular. See the list of irregular verbs on p142.

Present	→	Past
am/is/are		was/were
go		went
come		came
have		had
make		made
see		saw
buy		bought
say		said
find		found
do		did

UNIT 10

10.1 Past Simple positive

1 Regular verbs add -ed or -d in the Past Simple.

Present	→	Past
play		played
watch		watched
listen		listened
turn		turned
change		changed

❶ Remember: Many common verbs are irregular.

go	→	**went**
see	→	**saw**
have	→	**had**

See the list of irregular verbs on p142.

2 The form is the same for all persons.

I You He/She/It We They	listened to music. went to work. had lunch.

10.2 Past Simple questions and negatives

❶ Present do/does → Past did
What time **does** he usually get up?
What time **did** he get up yesterday?

Questions with question words

Where	did	I you he/she/it we they	go?

Negative

I You He/She/It We They	didn't	go shopping. see the film.

Yes/No questions and short answers

Did they play football?	Yes, they did.
Did you have a good time?	No, I didn't.

UNIT 11

▶ 11.1 can

Positive

I You He/She/It We They	can	swim. drive. cook. run fast.

Negative

I You He/She/It We They	can't	draw. speak German. play golf.

Questions with question words

What		you do?
When	can	I go home?
How many languages		he speak?

Yes/No questions and short answers

Can you swim?	Yes, I can.
Can he play tennis?	No, he can't.

▶ 11.2 Modal verbs

Can is a modal verb. We don't use *do/does/don't/doesn't* with *can*.

I can't swim.	NOT	*I don't can swim.*
Can you cook?	NOT	*Do you can cook?*
She can't speak Spanish.	NOT	*She doesn't can …*
They can't dance.	NOT	*They don't can …*

▶ 11.3 Adverbs

1 Adverbs give more information about verbs.
   go **fast**   draw **well**   sing **beautifully**

2 Notice the word order.
   *You **speak** English **well**.*   NOT   *You speak well English.*
   *He **drives** his car **fast**.*   NOT   *He drives fast his car.*

3 Regular adverbs end in -ly.

Adjective	→	Adverb
fluent		*fluent**ly***
beautiful		*beautiful**ly***
slow		*slow**ly***
careful		*careful**ly***
usual		*usual**ly***

4 Some adverbs are irregular.

Adjective	→	Adverb
good		**well**
fast		**fast**
late		**late**
early		**early**
hard		**hard**

UNIT 12

▶ 12.1 would like

1 We use *would like* to ask for things.

Positive

I You He/She We They	'd like a cup of tea.

2 We use *Would … like?* to offer things.

Question

Would	you he/she they	like some cake?

3 Look at the answers.

   Would you like a cup of tea?   *Yes, please.*
                                       No, thank you.

   We use *would like*, not *want*, to be polite.
   I'd like a coffee, please.   NOT   *I want a coffee.*

4 We can use *would like* with another verb.
   *Would you like **to go out** tonight?*
   *What would you like **to do**?*

▶ 12.2 some and any

1 We use *some* in positive sentences.

I'd like There's We have	some	ham. cheese. books.

2 We use *any* in questions.

Is there Do you have Are there	any	ham? money? people?

3 We use *any* in negatives.

There isn't We don't have There aren't	any	bread. friends. books.

4 We use *some* when we offer things or ask for things.

Would you like Can I have	some	wine? cheese?

▶ 12.3 like and would like

1 We use *like* and *like doing* to talk about things we always like.
   *I **like** coffee.*   (= I always enjoy coffee.)
   *She **likes** swimming in summer.*
   *What do you **like** doing at the weekend?*

2 We use *would like* to talk about things we want now or soon.
   *I'**d like** a cup of tea.*   (= I want a cup of tea now or soon.)
   *She's hot. She'**d like** to go swimming.*
   *What **would** you **like** to do tonight?*

UNIT 13

 13.1 Present Continuous

Positive

I	am	
He She It	is	working.
You We They	are	

Negative

I	'm not	
He She It	isn't	working.
You We They	aren't	

Questions with question words

	am I	
What	are you are we are they	wearing?
	is he is she	

Yes/No **questions and short answers**

Are you wearing jeans?	Yes, I am. No, I'm not.
Is she reading a newspaper?	Yes, she is. No, she isn't.

 13.2 Present Simple and Present Continuous

1 We use the Present Simple to talk about actions that are true for all time or a long time.
*Hans **comes** from Germany.*
*I **love** you.*
*My father **works** in a bank.*
*I **get up** at 7.30 every day.*
*She **doesn't understand** French.*

2 We use the Present Continuous to talk about actions that last a short time. The actions are happening now.
*I usually wear jeans, but today I**'m wearing** a suit.*
*He**'s speaking** French to that man. He speaks French very well.*
*It**'s raining**.*
*They**'re swimming**.*

UNIT 14

 14.1 Future plans

Positive

I'm You're He's She's We're They're	going to Europe. leaving next week. flying on Sunday.

I'm You're He's She's We're They're	going to	see Buckingham Palace. have a tour of the city. stay in the Ritz hotel.

Questions

Where When Where Who	are you	going on holiday? leaving? staying? going with?

Where What	are you going to	stay? do?

Word list

Here is a list of most of the new words in the units of *New Headway Beginner third edition* Student's Book.

adj = adjective	*n* = noun
adv = adverb	*pl* = plural
conj = conjunction	*prep* = preposition

pron = pronoun	
v = verb	
infml = informal	

 UNIT 1

and *conj* /ænd/, /ənd/

bag *n* /bæg/
book *n* /bʊk/
bus *n* /bʌs/
Bye! /baɪ/

camera *n* /ˈkæmrə/
car *n* /kɑː(r)/
coffee *n* /ˈkɒfi/
computer *n* /kəmˈpjuːtə(r)/
cup *n* /kʌp/

day *n* /deɪ/

English *adj, n* /ˈɪŋglɪʃ/
everyday *adj* /ˈevrideɪ/

fine *adj* /faɪn/
first name *n* /ˈfɜːst ˌneɪm/

Good afternoon! /gʊd ˌɑːftəˈnuːn/
Good morning! /gʊd ˈmɔːnɪŋ/
Good night! /gʊdˈnaɪt/
Goodbye! /gʊdˈbaɪ/

hamburger *n* /ˈhæmbɜːgə(r)/
Have a nice day! /ˌhæv ə naɪs ˈdeɪ/
hello *n* /helˈəʊ/
house *n* /haʊs/
How are you? /ˌhaʊ ə ˈjuː/

lovely *adj* /ˈlʌvli/

my /maɪ/

name *n* /neɪm/
Nice to meet you. /ˌnaɪs tə ˈmiːt juː/

OK *adj* /ˌəʊ ˈkeɪ/

phone *n* /fəʊn/
photograph *n* /ˈfəʊtəgrɑːf/
please /pliːz/

sandwich *n* /ˈsænwɪtʃ/
See you later! /ˌsiː ju ˈleɪtə(r)/
Sleep well! /ˈsliːp ˌwel/
surname *n* /ˈsɜːneɪm/

tea *n* /tiː/
television *n* /ˈtelɪvɪʒn/
thank you /ˈθæŋkjuː/
thanks /θæŋks/
this *pron* /ˈðɪs/
today *n* /təˈdeɪ/

very well /ˌveri ˈwel/

what? /ˌwɒt/
with *prep* /wɪð/

your /jɔː(r)/

Numbers 1–10
one /wʌn/
two /tuː/
three /θriː/

four /fɔː(r)/
five /faɪv/
six /sɪks/
seven /ˈsevn/
eight /eɪt/
nine /naɪn/
ten /ten/

 UNIT 2

about *prep* /əˈbaʊt/
awful *adj* /ˈɔːfl/

beautiful *adj* /ˈbjuːtɪfl/
building *n* /ˈbɪldɪŋ/

centre *adj* /ˈsentə(r)/
cities *n pl* /ˈsɪtiz/
countries *n pl* /ˈkʌntriz/

doctor *n* /ˈdɒktə(r)/

fantastic *adj* /fænˈtæstɪk/
find *v* /faɪnd/
from *prep* /frɒm/

hear *v* /hɪə(r)/
her /hɜː(r)/
his /hɪz/
hospital *n* /ˈhɒspɪtl/
how old? /haʊ ˈəʊld/

look at (sth) *v* /ˈlʊk ət/

map *n* /mæp/
married *adj* /ˈmærid/

on holiday /ɒn ˈhɒlədeɪ/

people *n pl* /ˈpiːpl/

really good *adj* /ˌriːəli ˈgʊd/

school *n* /skuːl/

these *pron* /ðiːz/
too *adv* /tuː/

weather *n* /ˈweðə(r)/
where? *adv* /weə(r)/
world *n* /wɜːld/

Countries
Australia *n* /ɒˈstreɪliə/
Brazil *n* /brəˈzɪl/
Canada *n* /ˈkænədə/
China *n* /ˈtʃaɪnə/
Egypt *n* /ˈiːdʒɪpt/
England *n* /ˈɪŋglənd/
France *n* /frɑːns/
Hungary *n* /ˈhʌŋgəri/
Italy *n* /ˈɪtəli/
Japan *n* /dʒəˈpæn/
Russia *n* /ˈrʌʃə/
Spain *n* /speɪn/
the United States *n pl*
  /ðə juːˌnaɪtɪd ˈsteɪts/

Numbers 11–30

eleven /ɪ'levn/ _____

twelve /twelv/ _____

thirteen /θɜ:'ti:n/ _____

fourteen /fɔ:'ti:n/ _____

fifteen /fɪf'ti:n/ _____

sixteen /sɪks'ti:n/ _____

seventeen /sevn'ti:n/ _____

eighteen /eɪ'ti:n/ _____

nineteen /naɪn'ti:n/ _____

twenty /'twenti/ _____

twenty-one /ˌtwenti'wʌn/ _____

twenty-two /ˌtwenti'tu:/ _____

twenty-three /ˌtwenti'θri:/ _____

twenty-four /ˌtwenti'fɔ:(r)/ _____

twenty-five /ˌtwenti'faɪv/ _____

twenty-six /ˌtwenti'sɪks/ _____

twenty-seven /ˌtwenti'sevn/ _____

twenty-eight /ˌtwenti'eɪt/ _____

twenty-nine /ˌtwenti'naɪn/ _____

thirty /'θɜ:ti/ _____

UNIT 3

address *n* /ə'dres/ _____

all *adv* /ɔ:l/ _____

America *n* /ə'merɪkə/ _____

another *pron* /ə'nʌðə(r)/ _____

audition *n* /ɔ:'dɪʃn/ _____

band *n* /bænd/ _____

boy *n* /bɔɪ/ _____

brother *n* /'brʌðə/ _____

builder *n* /'bɪldə(r)/ _____

bus driver *n* /'bʌs ˌdraɪvə(r)/ _____

businessman *n* /'bɪznəsmæn/ _____

excited *adj* /ɪk'saɪtɪd/ _____

excuse me /ɪk'skju:z ˌmi:/ _____

forty /'fɔ:ti/ _____

good luck /ɡʊd 'lʌk/ _____

Great! *adv* /ɡreɪt/ _____

happy *adj* /'hæpi/ _____

here *adv* /hɪə(r)/ _____

Hi /haɪ/ _____

I don't understand
  /aɪ ˌdəʊnt ʌndə'stænd/ _____

I'm sorry /aɪm 'sɒri/ _____

interesting *adv* /'ɪntrəstɪŋ/ _____

interview *n* /'ɪntəvju:/ _____

Ireland *n* /'aɪələnd/ _____

job *n* /dʒɒb/ _____

live *v* /lɪv/ _____

magazine *n* /ˌmæɡə'zi:n/ _____

now *adv* /naʊ/ _____

nurse *n* /nɜ:s/ _____

on tour *n* /ɒn 'tʊə(r)/ _____

other *adj* /'ʌðə(r)/ _____

over there /ˌəʊvə 'ðeə/ _____

personal information *n*
  /ˌpɜ:sənl ɪnfə'meɪʃn/ _____

phone number *n* /'fəʊn ˌnʌmbə(r)/ _____

police officer *n* /pə'li:s ˌɒfɪsə(r)/ _____

same *adj* /seɪm/ _____

Scotland *n* /'skɒtlənd/ _____

shop assistant *n* /'ʃɒp əˌsɪstənt/ _____

singer *n* /'sɪŋə/ _____

sorry /'sɒri/ _____

station *n* /'steɪʃn/ _____

Sweden *n* /'swi:dn/ _____

thanks a lot /ˌθæŋks ə 'lɒt/ _____

tired *n* /'taɪəd/ _____

town centre *n* /ˌtaʊn 'sentə(r)/ _____

very *adj* /'veri/ _____

well *n* /wel/ _____

winner *n* /'wɪnə(r)/ _____

yet *adv* /jet/ _____

UNIT 4

a lot of /ə 'lɒt əv/ _____

accountant *n* /ə'kaʊntənt/ _____

age *n* /eɪdʒ/ _____

bank manager *n* /'bæŋk ˌmænɪdʒə(r)/ _____

bank *n* /bæŋk/ _____

best friend *n* /ˌbest 'frend/ _____

big *adj* /bɪɡ/ _____

both *pron* /bəʊθ/ _____

boyfriend *n* /'bɔɪfrend/ _____

business card *n* /'bɪznɪs ˌkɑ:d/ _____

certainly *adv* /'sɜ:tənli/ _____

children *n pl* /'tʃɪldrən/ _____

college *n* /'kɒlɪdʒ/ _____

Come on! /ˌkʌm 'ɒn/ _____

company *n* /'kʌmpəni/ _____

connecting *v* /kə'nektɪŋ/ _____

dancing *n* /'dɑ:nsɪŋ/ _____

dictionary *n* /'dɪkʃənri/ _____

dog *n* /dɒɡ/ _____

evening *n* /'i:vnɪŋ/ _____

everybody *pron* /'evribɒdi/ _____

family tree *n* /ˌfæməli 'tri:/ _____

fans *n pl* /'fænz/ _____

football *n* /'fʊtbɔ:l/ _____

friends *n pl* /frendz/ _____

funny *adj* /'fʌni/ _____

Germany *n* /'dʒɜ:məni/ _____

girlfriend *n* /'gɜ:lfrend/ _____

give *v* /gɪv/ _____

goal *n* /gəʊl/ _____

good *adj* /gʊd/ _____

have *v* /hæv/ _____

home *n* /həʊm/ _____

hotel *n* /həʊ'tel/ _____

like *v* /laɪk/ _____

manager *n* /'mænɪdʒə(r)/

music *n* /'mjuːzɪk/

near *adj* /nɪə(r)/

new *adj* /njuː/

nice *adj* /naɪs/

north *adj* /nɔːθ/

notice *v* /'nəʊtɪs/

of course /əv 'kɔːs/

office *n* /'ɒfɪs/

our /aʊə(r)/

part of (something) *n* /'pɑːt əv/

part-time *adj* /ˌpɑːt 'taɪm/

police *n* /pə'liːs/

really *adj* /'riːəli/

rock 'n' roll *n* /ˌrɒkən'rəʊl/

small *adj* /smɔːl/

spell *v* /spel/

sport *n* /spɔːt/

sports centre *n* /'spɔːts ˌsentə(r)/

their /ðeə(r)/

together *adv* /tə'geðə(r)/

university *n* /ˌjuːnɪ'vɜːsəti/

us *pron* /ʌs/

village *n* /'vɪlɪdʒ/

want *v* /wɒnt/

The family

brother *n* /'brʌðə(r)/

daughter *n* /'dɔːtə(r)/

father *n* /'fɑːðə(r)/

husband *n* /'hʌzbənd/

mother *n* /'mʌðə(r)/

parents *n pl* /'peərənts/

sister *n* /'sɪstə(r)/

son *n* /sʌn/

wife *n* /waɪf/

▶ UNIT 5

actor *n* /'æktə(r)/

Arabic *n* /'ærəbɪk/

beer *n* /bɪə(r)/

blue *adj* /bluː/

cheese *n* /tʃiːz/

chocolate *n* /'tʃɒklət/

Coke *n* /kəʊk/

Come here! /ˌkʌm 'hɪə(r)/

count *v* /kaʊnt/

delicious *adj* /dɪ'lɪʃəs/

drama *n* /'drɑːmə/

drink *v* /drɪŋk/

eat *v* /iːt/

exciting *adj* /ɪk'saɪtɪŋ/

flat *n* /flæt/

food *n* /fuːd/

guys *n pl* /gaɪz/

how much? /ˌhaʊ 'mʌtʃ/

ice-cream *n* /'aɪskriːm/

identity *n* /aɪ'dentɪti/

languages *n pl* /'læŋgwɪdʒɪz/

list *n* /lɪst/

love *v* /lʌv/

Mexico *n* /'meksɪkəʊ/

millionaire *n* /ˌmɪljə'neə(r)/

nationalities *n pl* /ˌnæʃə'nælətiz/

orange *n* /'ɒrɪndʒ/

order *v* /'ɔːdə(r)/

pair (of) *n* /peə(r) (əv)/

party *n* /'pɑːti/

pizza *n* /'piːtsə/

play *v* /pleɪ/

Portugal *n* /'pɔːtʃʊgl/

pounds *n pl* /paʊndz/

prices *n pl* /'praɪsɪz/

restaurants *n pl* /'restrɒnts/

skiing *n* /'skiːɪŋ/

sometimes *adv* /'sʌmtaɪmz/

speak *v* /spiːk/

swimming *n* /'swɪmɪŋ/

Switzerland *n* /'swɪtsələnd/

tennis *n* /'tenɪs/

terrible *adj* /'terəbl/

the best *adj* /ðə 'best/

twin *n* /twɪn/

waiter *n* /'weɪtə(r)/

wine *n* /waɪn/

Nationalities

American /ə'merɪkən/

Brazilian /brə'zɪliən/

Chinese /tʃaɪ'niːz/

French /frentʃ/

German /'dʒɜːmən/

Italian /ɪ'tæliən/

Japanese /ˌdʒæpə'niːz/

Mexican /'meksɪkən/

Portuguese /ˌpɔːtʃʊ'giːz/

Spanish /'spænɪʃ/

Numbers 40–100

forty /'fɔːti/

fifty /'fɪfti/

sixty /'sɪksti/

seventy /'sevənti/

eighty /'eɪti/

ninety /'naɪnti/

one hundred /wʌn 'hʌndrəd/

▶ UNIT 6

all day *adj* /ˌɔːl 'deɪ/

always *adv* /'ɔːlweɪz/

artist *n* /'ɑːtɪst/

as usual /əz 'juːʒuəl/

at the weekend /ət ðə ˌwiːk'end/

aunt *n* /ɑːnt/

beach *n* /biːtʃ/

bed *n* /bed/

between *adv* /bɪˈtwiːn/

breakfast *n* /ˈbrekfəst/

businesswoman *n* /ˈbɪznɪswʊmən/

busy *adj* /ˈbɪzi/

buy *v* /baɪ/

come *v* /kʌm/

cook *v* /kʊk/

dad *n* /dæd/

dinner *n* /ˈdɪnə(r)/

director *n* /dəˈrektə(r)/

drive *v* /draɪv/

early *adv* /ˈɜːli/

eggs *n pl* /egz/

fill *v* /fɪl/

get home /ˌget ˈhəʊm/

get up /ˌget ˈʌp/

go out /ˌgəʊ ˈaʊt/

go shopping /ˌgəʊ ˈʃɒpɪŋ/

go to bed /ˌgəʊ tə ˈbed/

Good idea! /ˌgʊd aɪˈdɪə/

have a shower /ˌhæv ə ˈʃaʊə(r)/

in *prep* /ɪn/

Internet *n* /ˈɪntənet/

invite *v* /ɪnˈvaɪt/

leave *v* /liːv/

lesson *n* /ˈlesn/

life *n* /laɪf/

lifestyle *n* /ˈlaɪfstaɪl/

lunch *n* /lʌntʃ/

morning *n* /ˈmɔːnɪŋ/

never *adv* /ˈnevə(r)/

next *adj* /nekst/

o'clock *adv* /əˈklɒk/

often *adv* /ˈɒfn, ˈɒftən/

paint *v* /peɪnt/

piano *n* /piˈænəʊ/

questionnaire *n* /ˌkwestʃəˈneə(r)/

relax *v* /rɪˈlæks/

schooldays *n pl* /ˈskuːldeɪz/

sea *n* /siː/

seaside *n* /ˈsiːsaɪd/

shopping *n* /ˈʃɒpɪŋ/

shower *v, n* /ˈʃaʊə(r)/

(web)site *n* /(ˈweb)saɪt/

soon *adv* /suːn/

stay *v* /steɪ/

stop *v* /stɒp/

studio *n* /ˈstjuːdiəʊ/

taxi *n* /ˈtæksi/

time *n* /taɪm/

toast *n* /təʊst/

tomorrow *adv* /təˈmɒrəʊ/

TV *n* /ˌtiːˈviː/

typical *adj* /ˈtɪpɪkl/

(the) US *n pl* /juːˈes/

usually *adv* /ˈjuːʒuəli/

visit *n* /ˈvɪzɪt/

walk *n / v* /wɔːk/

watch *v* /wɒtʃ/

week *n* /wiːk/

when? /wen/

Days of the week

Monday *n* /ˈmʌndeɪ/

Tuesday *n* /ˈtjuːzdeɪ/

Wednesday *n* /ˈwenzdeɪ/

Thursday *n* /ˈθɜːzdeɪ/

Friday *n* /ˈfraɪdeɪ/

Saturday *n* /ˈsætədeɪ/

Sunday *n* /ˈsʌndeɪ/

UNIT 7

adore *v* /əˈdɔː(r)/

amazing *adj* /əˈmeɪzɪŋ/

anything *pron* /ˈeniθɪŋ/

aspirin *n* /ˈæsprɪn/

baby *n* /ˈbeɪbi/

because *prep* /bɪˈkɒz/

bedrooms *n pl* /ˈbedruːmz/

best *adj* /best/

black *n* /blæk/

boss *n* /bɒs/

café *n* /ˈkæfeɪ/

card *n* /kɑːd/

carrots *n pl* /ˈkærəts/

catch *v* /kætʃ/

cat *n* /kæt/

changing rooms *n pl* /ˈtʃeɪndʒɪŋ ˌruːmz/

cheap *adj* /tʃiːp/

chemist's *n* /ˈkemɪsts/

Chile *n* /ˈtʃɪli/

chips *n pl* /tʃɪps/

clothes *n pl* /kləʊðz/

coat *n* /kəʊt/

cold *adj* /kəʊld/

comfortable *adj* /ˈkʌmftəbl/

credit card *n* /ˈkredɪt ˌkɑːd/

Czech Republic *n* /ˌtʃek rɪˈpʌblɪk/

degrees *n pl* /dɪˈgriːz/

designer *n* /dɪˈzaɪnə(r)/

divorced *adj* /dɪˈvɔːst/

door *n* /dɔː(r)/

easy *adj* /ˈiːzi/

every /ˈevri/

expensive *adj* /ɪkˈspensɪv/

fashion house *n* /ˈfæʃn ˌhaʊs/

fast *adj* /fɑːst/

favourite *adj* /ˈfeɪvrɪt/

film director *n* /ˈfɪlm dəˌrektə(r)/

fog *n* /fɒg/

free time *n* /ˌfriː ˈtaɪm/

Frenchman *n* /ˈfrentʃmən/

friendly *adj* /ˈfrendli/

hat *n* /hæt/ _____

hate *v* /heɪt/ _____

homework *n* /ˈhəʊmwɜːk/ _____

hot *adj* /hɒt/ _____

how many? /ˌhaʊ ˈmeni/ _____

international *adj* /ˌɪntəˈnæʃnəl/ _____

jacket *n* /ˈdʒækɪt/ _____

jumper *n* /ˈdʒʌmpə(r)/ _____

kids *n pl* /kɪdz/ _____

large *adj* /lɑːdʒ/ _____

latte *n* /ˈlɑːteɪ/ _____

learn *v* /lɜːn/ _____

look *v* /lʊk/ _____

machine *n* /məˈʃiːn/ _____

meet *v* /miːt/ _____

mobile phones *n pl* /ˌməʊbaɪl ˈfəʊnz/ _____

model *n* /ˈmɒdl/ _____

money *n* /ˈmʌni/ _____

months *n pl* /mʌnθs/ _____

MP3 player *n* /ˌem piː ˈθriː ˌpleɪə(r)/ _____

neighbours *n pl* /ˈneɪbəz/ _____

newspaper *n* /ˈnjuːzpeɪpə(r)/ _____

no problem /ˈnəʊ ˌprɒbləm/ _____

October *n* /ɒkˈtəʊbə(r)/ _____

old *adj* /əʊld/ _____

over there /ˌəʊvə ˈðeə(r)/ _____

packet *n* /ˈpækɪt/ _____

parcel *n* /ˈpɑːsl/ _____

Pardon? /ˈpɑːdn/ _____

photographer *n* /fəˈtɒɡrəfə(r)/ _____

PIN *n* /ˈpɪn/ _____

place *n* /pleɪs/ _____

pop music *n* /ˈpɒp ˌmjuːzɪk/ _____

post *v* /pəʊst/ _____

Post Office *n* /ˈpəʊst ˌɒfɪs/ _____

postcard *n* /ˈpəʊstkɑːd/ _____

present *n* /ˈpreznt/ _____

programme *n* /ˈprəʊɡræm/ _____

railway station *n* /ˈreɪlweɪ ˌsteɪʃn/ _____

rain *n* /reɪn/ _____

red *adj* /red/ _____

return ticket *n* /rɪˈtɜːn ˌtɪkɪt/ _____

sad *adj* /sæd/ _____

salad *n* /ˈsæləd/ _____

scales *n pl* /skeɪlz/ _____

seafood *n* /ˈsiːfuːd/ _____

shampoo *n* /ʃæmˈpuː/ _____

shoes *n pl* /ʃuːz/ _____

shops *n pl* /ʃɒps/ _____

shows *n pl* /ʃəʊz/ _____

Singapore *n* /ˌsɪŋəˈpɔː(r)/ _____

single ticket *n* /ˈsɪŋɡl ˌtɪkɪt/ _____

song *n* /sɒŋ/ _____

stamp *n* /stæmp/ _____

Swedish *adj* /ˈswiːdɪʃ/ _____

take away *n* /ˈteɪkəweɪ/ _____

teach *v* /tiːtʃ/ _____

that *pron* /ðæt/ _____

toothpaste *n* /ˈtuːθpeɪst/ _____

town *n* /taʊn/ _____

train *n* /treɪn/ _____

try on *v* /traɪ ɒn/ _____

T-shirt *n* /ˈtiːʃɜːt/ _____

understand *v* /ˌʌndəˈstænd/ _____

very much /ˌveri ˈmʌtʃ/ _____

website *n* /ˈwebsaɪt/ _____

wet *adj* /wet/ _____

white *adj* /waɪt/ _____

who? /huː/ _____

why? /waɪ/ _____

wonderful *adj* /ˈwʌndəfl/ _____

wrong *adj* /rɒŋ/ _____

yellow *adj* /ˈjeləʊ/ _____

 ## UNIT 8

alarm clock *n* /əˈlɑːm ˌklɒk/ _____

any *pron* /ˈeni/ _____

armchair *n* /ˈɑːmtʃeə(r)/ _____

autumn *n* /ˈɔːtəm/ _____

bathroom *n* /ˈbɑːθruːm/ _____

border *n* /ˈbɔːdə(r)/ _____

bus station *n* /ˈbʌs ˌsteɪʃn/ _____

car keys *n pl* /ˈkɑː ˌkiːz/ _____

car park *n* /ˈkɑː ˌpɑːk/ _____

church *n* /tʃɜːtʃ/ _____

cinema *n* /ˈsɪnəmə/ _____

cooker *n* /ˈkʊkə(r)/ _____

cosmopolitan *adj* /ˌkɒzməˈpɒlɪtən/ _____

cycling *n* /ˈsaɪklɪŋ/ _____

desk *n* /desk/ _____

dining room *n* /ˈdaɪnɪŋ ˌruːm/ _____

directions *n* /dəˈrekʃnz/ _____

drawer *n* /drɔː(r)/ _____

DVD player *n* /ˌdiː viː ˈdiː ˌpleɪə(r)/ _____

excellent *adj* /ˈeksələnt/ _____

ferry *n* /ˈferi/ _____

festivals *n pl* /ˈfestɪvlz/ _____

fishing *n* /ˈfɪʃɪŋ/ _____

floor *n* /flɔː(r)/ _____

fresh *adj* /freʃ/ _____

fridge *n* /frɪdʒ/ _____

furniture *n* /ˈfɜːnɪtʃə(r)/ _____

games *n pl* /ɡeɪmz/ _____

golf *n* /ɡɒlf/ _____

home town *n* /ˌhəʊm ˈtaʊn/ _____

Indian *adj* /ˈɪndiən/ _____

Internet café *n* /ˈɪntənet ˌkæfeɪ/ _____

kinds of /ˈkaɪndz əv/ _____

kitchen *n* /ˈkɪtʃn/ _____

lamp *n* /læmp/ _____

laptop *n* /ˈlæptɒp/ _____

left /ˈleft/ _____

living room *n* /ˈlɪvɪŋ ˌruːm/ _____

mean *adj* /miːn/ _____

meetings *n pl* /ˈmiːtɪŋz/ _____

miles *n pl* /maɪlz/ _____

minutes *n pl* /'mɪnɪts/

modern *adj* /'mɒdn/

more *pron* /mɔ:(r)/

mountain *n* /'maʊntən/

need *v* /ni:d/

newsagent's *n* /'nju:zeɪdʒənts/

next to *prep* /'nekst tu:, tə/

night *n* /naɪt/

opera *n* /'ɒprə/

park *n* /pɑ:k/

posters *n pl* /'pəʊstəz/

pub *n* /pʌb/

quick *adj* /kwɪk/

right *adj* /raɪt/

rooms *n pl* /ru:mz/

run *v* /rʌn/

sailing *n* /seɪlɪŋ/

signs *n pl* /saɪnz/

sky *n* /skaɪ/

slow *adj* /sləʊ/

snowboarding *n* /'snəʊbɔ:dɪŋ/

sofa *n* /'səʊfə/

some /sʌm/

spectacular *adj* /spek'tækjələ(r)/

sports bag *n* /'spɔ:ts ˌbæg/

spring *n* /sprɪŋ/

straight on /ˌstreɪt 'ɒn/

summer *n* /'sʌmə(r)/

sunbathe *v* /'sʌnbeɪð/

sunbathing *n* /'sʌnbeɪðɪŋ/

sunny *adj* /'sʌni/

supermarket *n* /'su:pəmɑ:kɪt/

telephone *n* /'telɪfəʊn/

Thai *adj* /taɪ/

theatre *n* /'θɪətə(r)/

tidy *adj* /'taɪdi/

toilet *n* /'tɔɪlət/

trainers *n pl* /'treɪnəz/

travel *v* /'trævl/

trolley bus *n* /'trɒli ˌbʌs/

turn *v* /tɜ:n/

under *prep* /'ʌndə(r)/

walls *n pl* /wɔ:lz/

warm *adj* /wɔ:m/

water sports *n* /'wɔ:tə ˌspɔ:ts/

winter *n* /'wɪntə(r)/

▶ UNIT 9

art *n* /'ɑ:t/

Austria *n* /'ɒstriə/

back *n* /bæk/

birthday *n* /'bɜ:θdeɪ/

born *v* /bɔ:n/

Canadian *adj* /kə'neɪdiən/

charity shop *n* /'tʃærəti ˌʃɒp/

colourful *adj* /'kʌləfl/

dear *adj* /dɪə(r)/

do *v* /du:/

eldest *adj* /'eldɪst/

expert *n* /'ekspɜ:t/

famous *adj* /'feɪməs/

film *n* /fɪlm/

film company *n* /'fɪlm ˌkʌmpəni/

fingerprint *n* /'fɪŋgəprɪnt/

for sale /fə'seɪl/

gallery *n* /ˌgæləri/

go *v* /gəʊ/

good time /ˌgʊd 'taɪm/

grandfather *n* /'grænfɑ:ðə(r)/

grandmother *n* /'grænmʌðə(r)/

gym *n* /dʒɪm/

happy birthday /ˌhæpi 'bɜ:θdeɪ/

horrible *adj* /'hɒrəbl/

housework *n* /'haʊswɜ:k/

Irish *adj* /'aɪrɪʃ/

last year /ˌlɑ:st 'jɪə(r)/

make *v* /meɪk/

mess *n* /mes/

most /məʊst/

musician *n* /mju'ʒɪʃn/

next year /ˌnekst 'jɪə(r)/

older *adj* /'əʊldə(r)/

Pakistan *n* /ˌpækɪ'stæn/

pay *v* /peɪ/

politician *n* /ˌpɒlə'tɪʃn/

princess *n* /ˌprɪn'ses/

racing driver *n* /'reɪsɪŋ ˌdraɪvə(r)/

real *adj* /'ri:əl/

rich *adj* /rɪtʃ/

Saudi Arabia *n* /ˌsaʊdi ə'reɪbiə/

scientist *n* /'saɪəntɪst/

see *v* /si:/

singer *n* /'sɪŋə(r)/

south *adj* /saʊθ/

still *adj* /stɪl/

story *n* /'stɔ:ri/

thousand *n* /'θaʊzənd/

TV company *n* /ˌti: 'vi: ˌkʌmpəni/

uncle *n* /'ʌŋkl/

writer *n* /'raɪtə(r)/

year *n* /jɪə(r)/

yesterday *adv* /'jestədeɪ/

Months of the year

January *n* /dʒænjuəri/

February *n* /'februəri/

March *n* /mɑ:tʃ/

April *n* /'eɪprəl/

May *n* /meɪ/

June *n* /dʒu:n/

July *n* /dʒu'laɪ/

August *n* /'ɔ:gəst/

September *n* /sep'tembə(r)/

October *n* /ɒk'təʊbə(r)/

November *n* /nəʊ'vembə(r)/

December *n* /dɪ'sembə(r)/

Ordinal numbers

first *adj* /fɜːst/
second *adj* /ˈsekənd/
third *adj* /θɜːd/
fourth *adj* /fɔːθ/
fifth *adj* /fɪfθ/
sixth *adj* /sɪksθ/
seventh *adj* /ˈsevnθ/
eighth *adj* /eɪtθ/
ninth *adj* /naɪnθ/
tenth *adj* /tenθ/
eleventh *adj* /ɪˈlevənθ/
twelfth *adj* /twelfθ/
thirteenth *adj* /ˌθɜːˈtiːnθ/
fourteenth *adj* /ˌfɔːˈtiːnθ/
fifteenth *adj* /ˌfɪfˈtiːnθ/
sixteenth *adj* /ˌsɪksˈtiːnθ/
seventeenth *adj* /ˌsevnˈtiːnθ/
eighteenth *adj* /ˌeɪˈtiːnθ/
nineteenth *adj* /ˌnaɪnˈtiːnθ/
twentieth *adj* /ˈtwentiəθ/
thirtieth *adj* /ˈθɜːtiəθ/

UNIT 10

ago *adv* /əˈɡəʊ/
at *prep* /æt, ət/
bus tour *n* /ˈbʌs ˌtʊə(r)/
camping *n* /ˈkæmpɪŋ/
castle *n* /ˈkɑːsl/
cathedral *n* /kəˈθiːdrəl/
clean *v* /kliːnd/
coffee bar *n* /ˈkɒfi ˌbɑː(r)/
dance *n* /dɑːns/
date *n* /deɪt/
diner *n* /ˈdaɪnə(r)/
enjoy *v* /ɪnˈdʒɔɪ/
free *adj* /friː/
get *v* /ɡet/
horse riding *n* /ˈhɔːs ˌraɪdɪŋ/
ice-skating *n* /ˈaɪs ˌskeɪtɪŋ/
India *n* /ˈɪndiə/
interested *n* /ˈɪntrəstɪd/
lake *n* /leɪk/
last *adj* /lɑːst/
late *adj / adv* /ˌleɪt/
leisure activity *n* /ˈleʒə(r) ækˌtɪvəti/
listened *v* /ˈlɪsnd/
lots *pron* /lɒts/
lucky *adj* /ˈlʌki/
market *n* /ˈmɑːkɪt/
meal *n* /miːl/
milk *n* /mɪlk/
much *pron* /mʌtʃ/
museum *n* /mjuˈziːəm/
once *adv* /wʌns/
orange juice *n* /ˈɒrɪndʒ ˌdʒuːs/

pasta *n* /ˈpæstə/
playing cards *n pl* /ˈpleɪɪŋ ˌkɑːdz/
Really? /ˈriːəli/
relaxing *adj* /rɪˈlæksɪŋ/
roast beef *n* /ˌrəʊst ˈbiːf/
rugby *n* /ˈrʌɡbi/
show *v* /ʃəʊ/
sightseeing *n* /ˈsaɪtsiːɪŋ/
sit *v* /ˈsɪt/
skiing *n* /ˈskiːɪŋ/
special *adj* /ˈspeʃl/
square *n* /skweə(r)/
start *v* /stɑːt/
sun *n* /sʌn/
swimming pool *n* /ˈswɪmɪŋ ˌpuːl/
tour *n* /tʊə(r)/
tourist *n* /ˈtʊərɪst/
tourist office *n* /ˈtʊərɪst ˌɒfɪs/
villa *n* /ˈvɪlə/
walk *v* /ˈwɔːk/
weekend *n* /ˌwiːkˈend/
windsurfing *n* /ˈwɪndsɜːfɪŋ/
zoo *n* /zuː/

UNIT 11

a little bit /ə ˈlɪtl ˌbɪt/
accident *n* /ˈæksɪdənt/
act *v* /ækt/
afraid *adj* /əˈfreɪd/
airport *n* /ˈeəpɔːt/
also *adv* /ˈɔːlsəʊ/
anywhere *adv* /ˈeniweə(r)/
architect *n* /ˈɑːkɪtekt/
Argentina *n* /ˌɑːdʒənˈtiːnə/
arm *n* /ɑːm/
athlete *n* /ˈæθliːt/
barbecue *n* /ˈbɑːbɪkjuː/
beef *n* /biːf/
better *adj* /ˈbetə(r)/
bill *n* /bɪl/
blog *n* /blɒg/
boring *adj* /ˈbɔːrɪŋ/
button *n* /ˈbʌtn/
cake *n* /keɪk/
can *v* /kæn/
chat *v* /tʃæt/
chess *n* /tʃes/
communicate *v* /kəˈmjuːnɪkeɪt/
computer games *n pl*
/kəmˈpjuːtə ˌɡeɪmz/
continue *v* /kənˈtɪnjuː/
dangerous *adj* /ˈdeɪndʒərəs/
defense *n* /dɪˈfens/
department *n* /dɪˈpɑːtmənt/
draw *v* /drɔː/
endless *adj* /ˈendləs/
everything *pron* /ˈevriθɪŋ/

farmer n /ˈfɑːmə(r)/

film star n /ˈfɪlm ˌstɑː(r)/

fluently adj /ˈfluːəntli/

fly v /flaɪ/

football player n /ˈfʊtbɔːl ˌpleɪə/

geography n /dʒiˈɒɡrəfi/

glass n /ɡlɑːs/

grandma n /ˈɡrænmɑː/

green adj /ɡriːn/

guitar n /ɡɪˈtɑː(r)/

help v /help/

history n /ˈhɪstri/

horse n /hɔːs/

hour n /ˈaʊə(r)/

hurt v /hɜːt/

interpreter n /ɪnˈtɜːprɪtə(r)/

jumbo jet n /ˌdʒʌmbəʊ ˈdʒet/

kind adj /kaɪnd/

lift v /lɪft/

lost adj /lɒst/

message n /ˈmesɪdʒ/

metres n pl /ˈmiːtəz/

millions n pl /ˈmɪljənz/

miss v /mɪs/

mostly adv /ˈməʊstli/

motor racing n /ˈməʊtə ˌreɪsɪŋ/

musical instrument n
  /ˌmjuːzɪkl ˈɪnstrəmənt/

network n /ˈnetwɜːk/

news n /njuːz/

offer v /ˈɒfə(r)/

passport n /ˈpɑːspɔːt/

pilot n /ˈpaɪlət/

planes n pl /pleɪnz/

pop group n /ˈpɒp ˌɡruːp/

possible adj /ˈpɒsəbl/

problem n /ˈprɒbləm/

push v /pʊʃ/

radio n /ˈreɪdiəʊ/

really well /ˌriːəli ˈwel/

request v /rɪˈkwest/

ride v /raɪd/

safe adj /seɪf/

science n /ˈsaɪəns/

scientist n /ˈsaɪəntɪst/

send v /send/

share v /ʃeə(r)/

slowly adj /ˈsləʊli/

something pron /ˈsʌmθɪŋ/

swim v /swɪm/

tall adj /tɔːl/

the Net n /ðə ˈnet/

ticket n /ˈtɪkɪt/

ticket machine n /ˈtɪkɪt məˌʃiːn/

tractor n /ˈtræktə(r)/

try v /traɪ/

turn off v /ˌtɜːn ˈɒf/

use v /juːz/

water n /ˈwɔːtə(r)/

What's the matter? /ˌwɒts ðə ˈmætə(r)/

worldwide adj /ˈwɜːldwaɪd/

young adj /jʌŋ/

UNIT 12

anyone pron /ˈeniwʌn/

Anything else? /ˌeniθɪŋ ˈels/

apple pie n /ˌæpl ˈpaɪ/

around /əˈraʊnd/

bar n /bɑː/

beans n pl /biːnz/

bike n /baɪk/

bookshop n /ˈbʊkʃɒp/

bottle n /ˈbɒtl/

bread n /bred/

cereal n /ˈsɪəriəl/

chicken n /ˈtʃɪkɪn/

chocolate cake n /ˈtʃɒklət ˌkeɪk/

coffee shop n /ˈkɒfi ˌʃɒp/

conditioner n /kənˈdɪʃənə(r)/

customers n pl /ˈkʌstəməz/

describe v /dɪˈskraɪb/

dessert n /dɪˈzɜːt/

diet n /ˈdaɪət/

dishes n pl /ˈdɪʃɪz/

dollars n pl /ˈdɒləz/

dry adj /draɪ/

feel v /fiːl/

first class adj /ˌfɜːst ˈklɑːs/

fish n /fɪʃ/

floors n pl /flɔːz/

follow v /tə ˈfɒləʊ/

followed by /ˈfɒləʊd baɪ/

forget v /fəˈɡet/

fruit n /fruːt/

garden n /ˈɡɑːdn/

gate n /ɡeɪt/

glass of wine n /ˌɡlɑːs əv ˈwaɪn/

hair n /heə(r)/

ham n /hæm/

immediately adv /ɪˈmiːdiətli/

jam n /dʒæm/

juice n /dʒuːs/

just adv /dʒʌst/

kilometres n pl /ˈkɪləmiːtəz/

little adj /ˈlɪtl/

lunch box n /ˈlʌntʃ ˌbɒks/

mains n pl /meɪnz/

marathon n /ˈmærəθən/

maybe adv /ˈmeɪbi/

mayonnaise n /ˌmeɪəˈneɪz/

meat n /miːt/

menu n /ˈmenjuː/

mineral water n /ˈmɪnərəl ˌwɔːtə(r)/

mixed salad n /ˌmɪkst ˈsæləd/

mobile phone *n* /ˌməʊbaɪl ˈfəʊn/

move into /ˌmuːv ˈɪntu, ɪntə/

nearly *adv* /ˈnɪəli/

normal *adj* /ˈnɔːml/

on the side /ˌɒn ðə ˈsaɪd/

onion *n* /ˌʌniən/

ordering *v* /ˈɔːdərɪŋ/

perhaps *adv* /pəˈhæps/

plate *n* /pleɪt/

polite *adj* /pəˈlaɪt/

programs *n* /ˈprəʊgræmz/

pull *v* /pʊl/

report *v* /rɪˈpɔːt/

rice *n* /raɪs/

salmon *n* /ˈsæmən/

second class *adj* /ˌsekənd/

service *n* /ˈsɜːvɪs/

side orders *n pl* /ˈsaɪd ˌɔːdəz/

siesta *n* /siˈestə/

silly *adj* /ˈsɪli/

Sir *n* /sɜː/

slices *n pl* /ˈslaɪsɪz/

smaller *adj* /ˈsmɔːlə(r)/

smallest *adj* /ˈsmɔːlɪst/

smile *n* /smaɪl/

smoke *v* /sməʊk/

snack *n* /snæk/

soup *n* /suːp/

sparkling *adj* /ˈspɑːklɪŋ/

stand *v* /stænd/

starters *n* /ˈstɑːtəz/

sugar *n* /ˈʃʊgə(r)/

swap *v* /swɒp/

take photos *v* /ˌteɪk ˈfəʊtəʊz/

tapas *n* /ˈtæpəs/

thirsty *adj* /ˈθɜːsti/

till *prep* /tɪl/

tomato *n* /təˈmɑːtəʊ/

too many /ˌtuː ˈmeni/

too much /ˌtuː ˈmʌtʃ/

US dollars *n pl* /ˌjuː es ˈdɒləz/

vegetable *n* /ˈvedʒtəbl/

wait *v* /weɪt/

waitress *n* /ˈweɪtrəs/

world *n* /ˈwɜːld/

UNIT 13

actions *n pl* /ˈækʃnz/

angry *adj* /ˈæŋgri/

apartments *n pl* /əˈpɑːtmənts/

arrive *v* /əˈraɪv/

at the moment /ət ðə ˈməʊmənt/

boots *n pl* /buːts/

bored *adj* /bɔːd/

bring *v* /brɪŋ/

build *v* /bɪld/

business *n* /ˈbɪznəs/

call *v* /kɔːl/

carry *v* /ˈkæri/

choose *v* /tʃuːs/

close *v* /kləʊz/

cold /ˌkəʊld/

colours *n pl* /ˈkʌləz/

country house *n* /ˌkʌntri ˈhaʊs/

do well /ˌduː ˈwel/

dress *n* /dres/

end *adj* /end/

especially *adv* /ɪˈspeʃəli/

espresso *n* /eˈspresəʊ/

extra *adj* /ˈekstrə/

finish *n* /ˈfɪnɪʃ/

guess *v* /ges/

happening *n* /ˈhæpənɪŋ/

have a cold *v* /ˌhæv ə kəʊld/

headache *n* /ˈhedeɪk/

helping *n* /ˈhelpɪŋ/

homeless *n* /ˈhəʊmləs/

hostel *n* /ˈhɒstəl/

hungry *adj* /ˈhʌŋgri/

jeans *n pl* /dʒiːnz/

lose *v* /luːz/

open *v* /ˈəʊpən/

pleased *adj* /pliːzd/

poor *adj* /pɔː(r)/

private plane *n* /ˌpraɪvət ˈpleɪn/

public transport *n*
   /ˌpʌblɪk ˈtrænspɔːt/

put on *v* /pʊt ˈɒn/

remember *v* /rɪˈmembə(r)/

road *n* /rəʊd/

scarf *n* /skɑːf/

secret *n* /ˈsiːkrət/

sell *v* /sel/

shirt *n* /ʃɜːt/

shorts *n pl* /ʃɔːts/

skirt *n* /skɜːt/

sleep *v* /ˈsliːp/

socks *n pl* /sɒks/

someone *pron* /ˈsʌmwʌn/

spend money *v* /ˌspend ˈmʌni/

spend time *v* /ˌspend ˈtaɪm/

strawberry *n* /ˈstrɔːbəri/

successful *adj* /səkˈsesfl/

suit *n* /suːt/

take off *n* /ˈteɪk ɒf/

teenage *adj* /ˈtiːneɪdʒ/

tie *n* /taɪ/

trousers *n pl* /ˈtraʊzəz/

turn on *v* /ˌtɜːn ˈɒn/

turn off *v* /ˌtɜːn ˈɒf/

TV programme *n*
   /ˌtiː ˈviː ˌprəʊgræm/

video *n* /ˈvɪdiəʊ/

wear *v* /ˈweə/

window *n* /ˈwɪndəʊ/

win *v* /wɪn/

work *v* /wɜːk/

worried *v* /ˈwʌrid/

worth *adj* /wɜːθ/

Colours

black *adj* /blæk/

blue *adj* /bluː/

brown *adj* /braʊn/

green *adj* /griːn/

grey *adj* /greɪ/

red *adj* /red/

white *adj* /waɪt/

yellow *adj* /ˈjeləʊ/

UNIT 14

abroad *v* /əˈbrɔːd/

across *adv* /əˈkrɒs/

all year round /ˌɔːl jɪə ˈraʊnd/

along *prep* /əˈlɒŋ/

assistant *n* /əˈsɪstənt/

autoroute *n* /ˈɔːtəʊruːt/

balcony *n* /ˈbælkəni/

banana *n* /bəˈnɑːnə/

begin *v* /bɪˈgɪn/

Belgium *n* /ˈbeldʒəm/

biology *n* /baɪˈɒlədʒi/

party *n* /ˈpɑːti/

bistro *n* /ˈbiːstrəʊ/

boat *n* /bəʊt/

bridge *n* /brɪdʒ/

campus *n* /ˈkæmpəs/

canals *n pl* /kəˈnælz/

carefully *adj* /ˈkeəfəli/

check in *v* /ˌtʃek ˈɪn/

chef *n* /ʃef/

chemistry *n* /ˈkemɪstri/

connection *n* /kəˈnekʃn/

cost *n* /kɒst/

cruise *n* /kruːz/

developing countries *n pl*
  /dɪˌveləpɪŋ ˈkʌntriz/

doctors *n pl* /ˈdɒktəz/

east *n* /iːst/

economics *n* /ˌiːkəˈnɒmɪks/

Europe *n* /ˈjʊərəp/

events *n pl* /ɪˈvents/

exam *n* /ɪgˈzæm/

explain *v* /ɪkˈspleɪn/

expressions *n pl* /ɪkˈspreʃnz/

flight *n* /flaɪt/

future *n* /ˈfjuːtʃə(r)/

grow up /ˌgrəʊ ˈʌp/

gymnasium *n* /dʒɪmˈneɪziəm/

hope *v* /həʊp/

housewife *n* /ˈhaʊswaɪf/

how long? *adv* /ˌhaʊ ˈlɒŋ/

imagine *v* /ɪˈmædʒɪn/

important *n* /ɪmˈpɔːtənt/

jeep *n* /dʒiːp/

journalist *n* /ˈdʒɜːnəlɪst/

know *v* /nəʊ/

local *adj* /ˈləʊkl/

medicine *n* /ˈmedsn/

modern languages *n pl*
  /ˌmɒdn ˈlæŋgwɪdʒɪz/

motorbike *n* /ˈməʊtəbaɪk/

move *v* /muːv/

nearby *adj* /ˈnɪəbaɪ/

nervous *adj* /ˈnɜːvəs/

overnight *adv* /ˌəʊvəˈnaɪt/

painter *n* /ˈpeɪntə(r)/

Physics *n* /ˈfɪzɪks/

piece of information *n*
  /ˌpiːs əv ɪnfəˈmeɪʃn/

plans *n pl* /plænz/

pleasure *n* /ˈpleʒə(r)/

Psychology *n* /saɪˈkɒlədʒi/

quickly *adv* /ˈkwɪkli/

quite often /ˌkwaɪt ˈɒfn/

research company *n*
  /rɪˈsɜːtʃ ˌkʌmpəni/

revision *n* /rɪˈvɪʒn/

ride *n* /raɪd/

romantic *adj* /rəʊˈmæntɪk/

rucksack *n* /ˈrʌksæk/

safari *n* /səˈfɑːri/

Same to you /ˌseɪm tu ˈjuː/

Scottish *adj* /ˈskɒtɪʃ/

See you again soon
  /ˌsiː ju əgen ˈsuːn/

South Africa *n* /ˌsaʊθ ˈæfrɪkə/

souvenir *n* /ˌsuːvəˈnɪə(r)/

steak *n* /steɪk/

sunshine *n* /ˈsʌnʃaɪn/

tent *n* /tent/

there *adv* /ðeə(r)/

transport *n* /ˈtrænspɔːt/

trip *n* /trɪp/

tunnel *n* /ˈtʌnl/

women *n pl* /ˈwɪmɪn/

Zambia *n* /ˈzæmbiə/

Pairwork pages

UNIT 2 *p14*

PRACTICE

Cities and countries

2 Work with a partner.

Student A   Look at the photos on p14.
Student B   Look at the photos on this page.

Ask questions and write the answers.

> What's her name?
> Where's she from?

> What's his name?
> Where's he from?

His name's Gusztáv.
He's from Budapest.

Her name's Rosely.
She's from São Paulo.

Her name's Niki.
She's from London.

His name's Shakir.
He's from Cairo.

PRACTICE

Two different rooms

3 Work with a partner.

Student A	Look at the picture on p59.
Student B	Look at the picture on this page.

Your pictures are different. Talk about them to find differences.

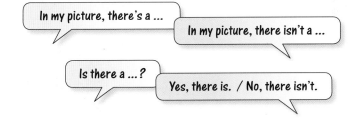

In my picture, there's a …

In my picture, there isn't a …

Is there a …?

Yes, there is. / No, there isn't.

Irregular verbs

Base form	Past Simple	Base form	Past Simple
be	was/were	lose	lost
begin	began	make	made
bring	brought	mean	meant
build	built	meet	met
buy	bought	pay	paid
can	could	put	put
catch	caught	read /ri:d/	read /red/
come	came	ride	rode
cost	cost	run	ran
do	did	say	said
draw	drew	see	saw
drink	drank	sell	sold
drive	drove	send	sent
eat	ate	sit	sat
feel	felt	sleep	slept
find	found	speak	spoke
fly	flew	spell	spelt
forget	forgot	spend	spent
get	got	stand	stood
give	gave	swim	swam
go	went	take	took
have	had	teach	taught
hear	heard	think	thought
know	knew	understand	understood
learn	learnt/learned	wear	wore
leave	left	win	win

Phonetic symbols

Consonants

1	/p/	as in	**pen**	/pen/
2	/b/	as in	**big**	/bɪg/
3	/t/	as in	**tea**	/ti:/
4	/d/	as in	**do**	/du:/
5	/k/	as in	**cat**	/kæt/
6	/g/	as in	**go**	/gəʊ/
7	/f/	as in	**four**	/fɔ:/
8	/v/	as in	**very**	/'veri/
9	/s/	as in	**son**	/sʌn/
10	/z/	as in	**zoo**	/zu:/
11	/l/	as in	**live**	/lɪv/
12	/m/	as in	**my**	/maɪ/
13	/n/	as in	**now**	/naʊ/
14	/h/	as in	**happy**	/'hæpi/
15	/r/	as in	**red**	/red/
16	/j/	as in	**yes**	/jes/
17	/w/	as in	**want**	/wɒnt/
18	/θ/	as in	**thanks**	/θæŋks/
19	/ð/	as in	**the**	/ðə/
20	/ʃ/	as in	**she**	/ʃi:/
21	/ʒ/	as in	**television**	/'telɪvɪʒn/
22	/tʃ/	as in	**child**	/tʃaɪld/
23	/dʒ/	as in	**German**	/'dʒɜ:mən/
24	/ŋ/	as in	**English**	/'ɪŋglɪʃ/

Vowels

25	/i:/	as in	**see**	/si:/
26	/ɪ/	as in	**his**	/hɪz/
27	/i/	as in	**twenty**	/'twenti/
28	/e/	as in	**ten**	/ten/
29	/æ/	as in	**bag**	/bæg/
30	/ɑ:/	as in	**father**	/'fɑ:ðə/
31	/ɒ/	as in	**hot**	/hɒt/
32	/ɔ:/	as in	**morning**	/'mɔ:nɪŋ/
33	/ʊ/	as in	**football**	/'fʊtbɔ:l/
34	/u:/	as in	**you**	/ju:/
35	/ʌ/	as in	**sun**	/sʌn/
36	/ɜ:/	as in	**learn**	/lɜ:n/
37	/ə/	as in	**letter**	/'letə/

Diphthongs (two vowels together)

38	/eɪ/	as in	**name**	/neɪm/
39	/əʊ/	as in	**no**	/nəʊ/
40	/aɪ/	as in	**my**	/maɪ/
41	/aʊ/	as in	**how**	/haʊ/
42	/ɔɪ/	as in	**boy**	/bɔɪ/
43	/ɪə/	as in	**hear**	/hɪə/
44	/eə/	as in	**where**	/weə/
45	/ʊə/	as in	**tour**	/tʊə/

OXFORD
UNIVERSITY PRESS

Great Clarendon Street, Oxford OX2 6DP

Oxford University Press is a department of the University of Oxford. It furthers the University's objective of excellence in research, scholarship, and education by publishing worldwide in

Oxford New York

Auckland Cape Town Dar es Salaam Hong Kong Karachi Kuala Lumpur Madrid Melbourne Mexico-City Nairobi New Delhi Shanghai Taipei Toronto

With offices in

Argentina Austria Brazil Chile Czech Republic France Greece Guatemala Hungary Italy Japan Poland Portugal Singapore South Korea Switzerland Thailand Turkey Ukraine Vietnam

OXFORD and OXFORD ENGLISH are registered trade marks of Oxford University Press in the UK and in certain other countries

© Oxford University Press 2011

The moral rights of the author have been asserted
Database right Oxford University Press (maker)

First published 2010

2015 2014 2013 2012 2011 2010

10 9 8 7 6 5 4 3 2

No unauthorized photocopying

ISBN: 978 0 19 471456 3

Printed in China

ACKNOWLEDGEMENTS

Illustrations by: Thea Brine pp.41, 89; Jonathan Burton p.86; Chris Boon p.61 (Canadian flag); Gill Button pp.6, 7, 18, 38 (James Bond), 46, 47, 50, 59, 70, 75, 83, 98 (cooking, driving etc), 102, 103, 110, 126, 141; Rowie Christopher Designs p.30; Claire Littlejohn pp.63, 79; Joe McLaren pp.11, 95, 104; Patrick Morgan/Debutart pp.14-15; Gavin Reece pp.38 (party), 52, 56, 57, 58, 68-9, 97, 98 (Nigel), 99; Martin Sanders p.60 (map); Kath Walker pp.32, 92, 96

Commissioned photography by: Gareth Boden pp.6, 7 (Pablo, Mika, Ben), 8, 9, 12, 13, 14 Rosely (middle), pp.15, 140 Rosely, 20, 22, p.23 male in pink shirt & female, 24, 27 Paddy McNab & family, 29 Antonia & Vince, 34, 35, 50, 54, 55, 72, 80 Oliver, Margaret, 81, 88, 89 balloons; Chris King p.73; Stephen Ogilvy p.42

The publisher would like to thank the following for their help with providing a location: The Biochemistry Building (Café); First Great Western (Oxford Railway Station); Four Pillars Hotel (Oxford Spires); Kendall Crescent Post Office; lizziejames; The North Wall Arts Centre; OUP Private Dining Room; The Oxford English Centre; Portabello Restaurant; Rowlands Pharmacy; St Barnabas' Primary School; The House; The Town Garden, North Parade; The Woodstock Road Deli (The Oxford Cheese Co.) With special thanks for help with location and models to: The Oxford English Centre.

We would also like to thank the following for permission to reproduce the following photographs: Alamy pp.13 (Karima/Bill Bachmann), 13 (Tatiana/Blaine Harrington III), 14 (Chinese woman/Redchopsticks.com LLC), 15 (Russian man/Russell Blake), 15 (American woman/i love images), 15 (Turkish man/Itani Images), 16 (Empire State building/MARKA), 17 (girl with helmet/Wolffy), 17 (woman drinking coffee/Alex Segre), 17 (man playing golf/i love images), 18 (teacher/Gabe Palmer), 21 (taxi driver/Patrik Jandak), 23 (old lady/Tony Hobbs), 23 (women carrying books/Adrian Sherratt), 25 (hospital/Peter Scholey), 26 (city/David R. Frazier Photolibrary, Inc.), 29 (older couple/Image Source Pink), 32 (football fan/John Simmons), 33 (American football player/Tetra Images), 37 (handbag/INSADCO Photography), 37 (coffee/Michael Snell), 37 (wine/Stockfolio), 39 (iphone/eyewave), 39 (beer/Cephas Picture Library), 40 (watch/Caro), 40 (ornate railway clock/Iain Masterton), 40 (clear alarm clock/studiomode), 40 (clock/Nick David), 44 (Cape Cod house/Jeff Greenberg), 44 (woman and dog on beach/Georgie Clarke), 44 (Woman artist/JupiterImages/Polka Dot), 53 (Golden Gate Bridge/Arco Images GmbH), 53 (houses/Jon Arnold Images Ltd), 57, 58 (man in yellow shirt/Queerstock, Inc.), 58 (man in yellow shirt/Queerstock, Inc.), 60 (fishermen/Danita Delimont), 60 (trolly bus/David Wei), 60 (sky train/Pep Roig), 60 (Kitsilano Beach/Ulana Switucha), 60 (skiers/Chris Cheadle), 62 (skyline/Pep Roig), 62 (couple/Morgan Lane Photography), 65 (silhouette of elderly man/Caro), 65 (silhouette of parents and child/Kirsty Pargeter), 65 (silhouette of mother and children/Yuri Maselov), 71 (birthday party/OJO Images Ltd), 74 (men eating/Andrew Fox), 76 (cards/Tony French), 76 (Girl on horse/John White Photos), 76 (walkers/Patrick Eden), 76 (rugby player/Paul Ridsdale), 77 (Tuscan houses/imagebroker), 77 (couple at airport/JupiterImages/Polka Dot), 78 (camping/All Canada Photos), 82 (tango dancers/Jon Arnold Images Ltd), 85 (Santiago/GlowImages), 85 (Lauren/Radius Images), 87 (tourists reading map/Richard Levine), 87 (office workers/Tetra Images), 87 (buying parking ticket/Chris Cooper-Smith), 90 (Jade/B.A.E. Inc.), 93 (Caroline/Amana Images inc.), 94 (waiter/JupiterImages/BananaStock), 101 (teenage boys/Photofusion Picture Library), 101 (elderly couple/Paul Baldesare), 103 (couple with boxes/Purestock), 106 (man with map/Colin Hawkins), 108 (doctors/Andres Rodriguez), 111 (waving at car/GoGo Images Corporation), 111 (waving at friends/Radius Images), 140 (chinese woman/Redchopsticks.com LLC), 141 (Russian man/Russell Blake), 141 (American woman/i love images), 141 (Egyptian man/Itani Images); Cadmium p.91 (fishing); Car Photo Library p.100 (Lamborghini); Carolyn Contino/BEI/Rex Features p.69 (Teri Horton with painting); Chris Boon p.29 (magazines), 37 (Oxford Dictionary), 40 (iPhone); Corbis UK Ltd. pp.13 (Yong/Justin Guariglia), 15 (man talking/Colorblind Images/Blend Images), 33 (man pulling face/Fancy/Veer), 37 (Cadillac/Car Culture), 44 (piano/James Mitchell/Zefa), 49 (children/M. Dominik/Zefa), 53 (Liberty Bell/Tetra Images), 57 (woman on phone/Fancy/Veer), 60/61 (Coal Harbor Vancouver/Jose Fuste Raga), 66 (Mozart/The Gallery Collection), 68 (Jackson Pollock/Rudolph Burckhardt/Sygma), 76 (soccer player/Randy Faris), 76 (flamenco dancer/Ilian Iliev/Lebrecht Music & Arts), 76 (biking/Jamie Kripke), 76 (tennis/Patrik Giardino), 76 (skier/Randy Faris), 76 (ice skater/Patrik Giardino), 76 (golf/Richard Schultz), 77 (ski lift/Jon Hicks), 80 (architect/Strauss/Curtis), 80 (athlete/Russell Glenister/Zefa), 82 (horse riding/Hugh Sitton/Zefa), 103 (headache/Jack Hollingsworth), 108 (family with car/Hans Neleman/Zefa), 108 (woman studying/Cultura), 111 (waving from train/Comstock Select); Getty Images pp.10 (house/David Oliver/Taxi), 13 (Kevin/Yellow Dog Productions), 16 (couple with umbrella/Comstock), 16 (New York traffic/Panoramic Images), 17 (boy with guitar/Ron Levine/Digital Vision), 23 (men with map/James Woodson), 26 (Oscar/Greg Ceo), 26 (Elena/Laurence Mouton/PhotoAlto), 26 (mature couple/David Sacks), 29 (dancer silhouette/Runstudio/Taxi), 36 (boys with surfboard/Hans Neleman), 36 (businessman/Matt Henry Gunther), 48 (Paris sketch/Eastnine Inc.), 48 (woman/Ryan McVay), 74 (sweeping floor/Yellow Dog Productions/Lifesize), 74 (shopping bags/David Woolley/Lifesize), 74 (homework/Comstock Images/Jupiterimages), 80 (pilot/Sascha Schuermann/AFP), 80 (interpreter/Dominique Faget/AFP), 85 (laptops/Ian McKinnell/Photographer's Choice), 87 (packing/Leukos/Photographer's Choice RF), 87 (helping woman to stand/Hola Images), 92 (Masumi/Antony Nagelmann/Taxi), 92 (dining table from above/Tom Schierlitz/The Image Bank), 93 (chicken salad/James Baigrie/Riser), 93 (paella/Michael Grimm/Riser), 93 (Adella/Jack Hollingsworth), 100 (big house/Altrendo travel), 100 (man in suit/Matthias Clamer/Stone), 100 (plane/© 2004 Katsuhiko Tokunaga/Check Six), 105 (older couple/Olivia Barr/Photonica), 111 (giving gift/Comstock Images), 111 (students/Digital Vision); Holly Mahoney p.19 (Ellie Green and friends); iStockphoto pp.10 (home office/Dean Turner), 10 (hamburger/Lise Gagne), 16 (central park), 85 (Charlotte), 90 (Mike), 90 (Kelly/Sheryl Griffin); Library of Congress p.64 (Jane Austen); Linographic p.10 (bag); Liz & John Soars pp.17 (toddler eating), 78 (beach); Martyn F. Chillmaid pp.85 (Oliver), 85 (Alan); Nikon p.37 (camera); Oxford University Press pp.10 (camera/Judith Collins), 13 (Laszlo/Gareth Boden), 13 (Simon/Image Source), 14 (English girl/Polka Dot Images), 21 (shop assistant/Chris King), 29 (couple in park), 37 (oranges), 39 (handbag/Stephen Hawkins), 53 (trolly car/Jon Arnold Images), 65 (young woman/Photodisc), 74 (cinema audience/Image 100), 74 (playing football), 76 (windsurfer/Photodisc), 76 (sailing boat/Ingram), 78 (walking/Melba Photo Agency), 78 (sightseeing/Image Source), 87 (couple talking/Chris King), 111 (broken pot/Richard Lewisohn/Image Source), 140 (English girl/Polka Dot Images); Photolibrary Group pp.7 (shaking hands), 13 (Hayley), 14 (Hungarian man), 14 (Australian man), 23 (coffee shop/BlueMoon Images), 29 (couple with guitar/Johner/Lars Tranquis), 33 (brother and sister/Jaume Gual), 37 (beer), 37 (Chicken fajitas/Frank Wieder Photography/Fresh Food Images), 92 (bento box), 107 (train/Claver Carroll), 140 (Hungarian Man), 140 (Australian man); Press Association Images pp.49 (catwalk/ABACA Press France), 66 (Shakespeare/PA WIRE), 66 (Andy Warhol/Associated Press), 66 (Michael Jackson/Associated Press), 67 (Benazir Bhutto/LANDOV), 67 (Marilyn Monroe), 67 (Ayrton Senna/Sutton Motorsports); Rex Features pp.32 (girl eating ice cream/OJO Images), 64 (Luciano Pavarotti/Reg Wilson), 66 (Princess Diana), 80 (farmer on tractor/WestEnd61); psd graphics.com p.13 (map); Robert Harding Picture Library pp.27 (fishing village, Ireland/Bruno Barbier), 36 (old people under tree/CuboImages), 36 (grape pickers/Upperhall Ltd); Science Photo Library pp.18 (doctor); Shutterstock pp.10 (television/Michael D Brown), 10 (telephone), 23 (asking directions/Factoria singular fotografia), 33 (tennis/Junial Enterprises), 39 (jeans), 76 (swimming/Schmid Christophe), 76 (fishing/Mikael Damkier), 85 (Edna/Martina Ebel); Toyota (GB) PLC p.10 (Toyota Prius); Studio 7 Designs p.13; Zooid Pictures pp.10 (book/Ned Coomes), 10 (photograph/Ned Coomes), 10 (bus/Taryn Cass), 10 (sandwich/Ned Coomes), 39 (sandwich/Ned Coomes), 39 (dictionary/Ned Coomes), 39 (chocolate).

Although every effort has been made to contact copyright holders before publication, this has not been possible in some cases. We apologise for any apparent infringement of copyright and if notified, the publisher will be pleased to rectify any errors or omissions at the earliest opportunity.